649.7
R722r

Raising a
Nonviolent Child

Yahweh examines the upright and the wicked,
the lover of violence he detests.
—Psalms 11:5 New Jerusalem Bible (NJB)

_____

So are the ways of everyone who gains by violence;
it takes away the life of its possessors.
—Proverbs 1:19 NJB

Raising a Nonviolent Child

John Rosemond

Andrews McMeel
Publishing

Kansas City

00 01 02 03 04 QUF 10 9 8 7 6 5 4 3 2

Library of Congress Cataloging-in-Publication Data

Rosemond, John K., 1947–
    Raising a nonviolent child / John Rosemond.
        p. cm.
    Includes index.
    ISBN 0-7407-0671-3 (hardcover)
    1. Children and violence—United States. 2. Violence in
children—United States. 3. Child rearing—United States.
4. Child psychology—United States. I. Title.
HQ784.V55 R66 2000
649'.7—dc21

                                        00-030502

Design and composition by Kelly & Company, Lee's Summit, Missouri

For the most wonderful Willie,
with whom all things are possible

Contents

Preface

First, I know the title is not grammatical. Well, it actually is, but only if this is a book about how to raise children who have proven to be peace-loving—which it is not. It is about raising children in such a way that they will eschew violence. Therefore, the title should be *Raising a Child to Be Nonviolent* or something of the sort. Forgive me. I pointed this out to my editor, but after some discussion we both agreed that, in this case, the ungrammatical was clear, concise, and more pleasing to the ears and eyes. So *Raising a Nonviolent Child* it is.

Second, an author is supposed to use the preface to justify the writing of the book in question, so here is my justification for writing *Raising a Nonviolent Child*.

A year-2000 survey conducted by the nonprofit group I Am Your Child and *Parents* magazine revealed the threat of violence done to or by a child is the number-one concern of America's parents. According to the survey, two out of every ten parents know a child who has been the victim of serious violence. More surprising, however, is the fact that *three* in ten parents are afraid their *own* children are capable of serious acts of violence. No such surveys were conducted forty years ago (when I was twelve), but had there been I daresay not *one* out of ten parents would have expressed similar worries.

Since 1965, the year I graduated from a very rough high school in suburban Chicago, the rate of child and teen violence has increased by a value of ten.

No one would be naïve enough to deny that today's children are committing acts of violence that parents of fifty years ago wouldn't have considered possible in their moments of wildest speculation.

The once-mischievous American child has become dangerous, to him- or herself and to others.

Efforts on the part of politicians, psychologists, clergy, and schools have failed to stem the rising tide of child violence. Furthermore, their well-intentioned efforts will continue to fail. There is only one group of people whose actions can be effective in this regard: parents.

This book was written as a To Arms! manual for parents who want to do their part to rehabilitate America's children. The rehabilitation will begin at home. *Your* home.

Thank you ...

WILLIE ROSEMOND is my most wonderful wife of thirty-two years. She put up with my writing yet another book, a project that took me away from her for a significant amount of time in 1999 and early 2000. She didn't complain once. She is truly a saint, my very own earth angel.

Julie Clark is a Richmond, Virginia, homemaker with a passion for research. Julie contributed generously of her time, talents, and energy to this book, doing what I don't have the patience to do.

Patrick Rosemond is one of my three grandsons. On a fateful day in September 1999 he hauled off and swatted me in the face. Like your daddy before you, Patrick, you are destined to give me great material.

DuBose (Bose) Ravenel is a High Point, North Carolina, pediatrician. He's also a member of Focus on the Family's Physician Resource Counsel and a leading figure in the national fight against antispanking legislation. His comments and guidance concerning the next-to-final draft were most helpful.

Sarah Hilton is an Alaska homemaker who gave freely of her time to do valuable research on the effects of media violence on children's behavior. Her efforts were indispensable to the final product.

Dell Computer, Microsoft, and America Online assisted ably in this project. Does anyone remember what the world was like before personal computers and the Internet?

My editors at the *Charlotte Observer* and the Knight-Ridder Wire have worked patiently with me over the years, trying to turn a hack into a writer. If they have not completely succeeded, it is only due to their student's limits.

All the folks at Andrews McMeel have been wonderfully supportive over the last twelve years and nine books. With regards to the present effort, my thanks go out especially to Tom Thornton, Chris Schillig, and Janet Baker.

Introduction

THE RATE OF child and teen violence has increased sharply since 1965, along with lay and professional concern over the problem. The tip of the iceberg consists of kids who commit violent crimes heinous enough to generate national media attention, kids like (age given at time of the incident):

- *Luke Woodham of Pearl, Mississippi.* On October 1, 1997, sixteen-year-old Woodham stabbed and killed his mother, then went to his high school and opened fire, killing two and wounding seven.
- *Michael Carneal of West Paducah, Kentucky.* On December 1, 1997, Carneal, fourteen, brought to school a gun he'd stolen from a neighbor and fired eight shots at an early morning student prayer meeting. The result was three dead, one paralyzed for life, and four wounded.
- *Mitchell Johnson and Andrew Golden of Jonesboro, Arkansas.* On March 24, 1998, thirteen-year-old Johnson and eleven-year-old Golden drove a stolen van filled with stolen weapons to a local middle school, where they set off the fire alarm and then ran for the cover of a nearby wooded ridge where they'd stashed their arsenal. As teachers and students filed out of the building, Johnson and Golden opened fire, killing four little girls and a teacher and wounding ten others.

- *Kip Kinkel of Springfield, Oregon.* On May 20, 1998, Kinkel, fifteen, killed his parents with an automatic pistol his father had bought for him. He then drove himself to his high school, where he walked into the cafeteria and began firing randomly at classmates with a semiautomatic rifle, killing two and wounding twenty-two.
- *Dylan Klebold and Eric Harris of Littleton, Colorado.* On April 20, 1999, seventeen-year-old Klebold and eighteen-year-old Harris went on a well-planned killing spree at Columbine High School, where they methodically murdered twelve students and a teacher before committing suicide in the cafeteria as police closed in.

In 1999, child psychologist and best-selling novelist Jonathan Kellerman (e.g., *When the Bough Breaks*) wrote a book, *Savage Spawn,* about young killers of this sort in which he called them psychopaths—impulsive, narcissistic, lacking in conscience and the ability to feel remorse, oriented to instant gratification. Psychopaths believe they deserve whatever they want and their self-centered ends justify even the most odious means imaginable. In short, a psychopath is the embodiment of evil. Scarier yet, psychopaths are, for all intents and purposes, immune to therapeutic efforts. From their point of view, they are not doing anything wrong. Wrong is getting caught. Therefore, they don't see any reason to change. Kellerman suggests that once a child psychopath becomes a cold-blooded killer, society's best recourse is to "lock him up till he dies." Strong words from a child psychologist, eh?

Psychologists and psychiatrists have had enough experience with psychopaths of all ages to know that disproportionate numbers of them were raised by people who themselves were psychopathic—

sexually promiscuous, violence-prone, masters of swindle. Psychopaths not only make bad role models, they are also dangerous caretakers of children. In fact, it could hardly be said that they *care* much at all for their children. Their overweening self-centeredness blinds them to the needs of their kids, so they have a habit of neglecting them. When frustrated, psychopaths often lose control. This, combined with a powerful need for instant gratification, disposes them to lash out violently at their children whenever their children irritate them. I'm talking about the sort of parent who thinks nothing about beating a toddler unconscious to make him stop crying. The abused and neglected child is at risk of never being able to form strong bonds of attachment. Empathy—sensitivity to other people's feelings—is absent from his emotional repertoire. He grows up also unable to *care* how other people feel, how his behavior affects others. Thus, psychopaths breed psychopaths.

Not all child psychopaths, however, have parents who are truly psychopathic themselves. The evidence suggests that a parent who is withdrawn, passive, remote—chronically depressed and therefore often neglectful, but not abusive—is likely to raise a child with an underdeveloped capacity to empathize with others and form close relationships. Such a child will probably be relatively passive and may see himself as a social victim. He may also become chronically depressed himself. He may never get angry enough to bust loose and go on a killing spree. But then again, he might.

At this point, the important thing to understand is that psychopathic or neglectful parents don't read parenting books. Self-improvement books are read by introspective people who obviously want to *improve* one aspect or another of their lives. Psychopaths lack the ability to be introspective, and it goes without saying they don't desire self-improvement. They don't think they need to

improve. They're already the epitome of creation. This book, therefore, was not written with psychopaths in mind.

The sort of parent who reads this book wants the best for his
or her children, wants to be the best parent he or she can possibly
be. This book is addressed to well-socialized moral people who,
like yourself, want to raise kids who become well-socialized moral
adults.

Don't heave too big a sigh of relief, though, because the fact that
you aren't psychopathic doesn't mean your child stands no chance
of ever becoming angry enough to do something violent to someone else or despairing enough to do something self-destructive. It is
significant to note that there's no real evidence that any of the children just listed were raised by psychopaths. What this means is that
caring, well-socialized parents can still produce little criminals. How
those seven children came to be capable of premeditated, cold-
blooded mass murder is a mystery. Almost certainly, they are psychopaths. To paraphrase Forrest Gump, "A psychopath is as a psychopath does." Are we ever going to know what morbid influences in
each of their lives "drove" them to kill? Perhaps not. Perhaps they
weren't driven at all. Maybe they were once normal kids raised in
fairly normal ways who, for reasons that will remain forever un-
known, made a pact with the devil. Who knows?

The tip of the child-violence iceberg—psychopathic children
going on premeditated killing sprees—is certainly a problem, but
it's not *the* problem. *The* problem is that America's children are becoming more violent. To repeat my first sentence: "The rate of
child and teen violence has increased sharply since 1965."

As reported in the *Archives of Pediatric and Adolescent Medi-
cine* (1995):

Adolescents are now experiencing the highest and most rapidly increasing rates of lethal and nonlethal violence. The increase in violence among youths 10 to 14 years of age is especially important and alarming.

It would be somewhat comforting to think this sharp increase was taking place exclusively among children of the underclass. Not so. While concentrated in America's inner cities, the increase in child violence is happening across the demographic spectrum. Between 1982 and 1991, the arrest rate for juveniles increased 93 percent for murder and 72 percent for aggravated assault. About three million thefts and violent crimes occur on or near some school campus each year, representing nearly 16,000 incidents per day. By the best estimate, 20 percent of high school students carry some sort of weapon (gun, knife, razor) with them to school on a regular basis. Not all the crimes in question are committed by kids from "bad" neighborhoods. More and more kids from "good" neighborhoods are acting out in antisocial ways—committing vandalism, armed robbery, grand theft, rape, and murder.

Not all youthful offenders are true psychopaths. Most are otherwise okay kids who've been led astray or allowed to go astray. Just as an otherwise law-abiding adult can do something criminal without *being* a criminal in the strict sense of the term, a child can do something psychopathic without being a true psychopath. Another facet of the problem is that more and more otherwise "normal" kids from "normal" families are doing psychopathic sorts of things—violent, antisocial things. Much of the violence in question never shows up in statistics. Therefore, anecdotes will have to tell the tale.

- Teachers who've taught since the 1960s report that children have become considerably more aggressive—verbally and physically—over that period of time. Schoolyard bullies are more in evidence and less cautious about who witnesses their dirty work. In this case, some corroborating evidence exists. On September 7, 1999, *USA Today* reported a survey that revealed 40 percent of children in grades six through twelve have threatened to physically hurt another student at school. Nearly 20 percent of children surveyed reported they had hit another student while at school, and 25 percent reported feeling physically intimidated by another student. Said the authors of the survey, "The findings add to the growing body of evidence that bullying is widespread in the nation's schools."

- By all reports, sibling conflict has become more violent. Fifty years ago, siblings fought mostly with words, by refusing to share, and by cheating during games. Back then, it was relatively rare to run across siblings who were *trying* to hurt one another. Unfortunately, this is anything but rare today. In light of the following, however, the rise of sibling-on-sibling violence is not surprising.

- What was unheard of forty years ago—children hitting their parents—has become familiar. In many cases these are kids whose parents are caring, conscientious, and responsible. My sense, acquired in the course of conversations with parents around the country who admit to being hit by their kids, is that the overwhelming majority of these kids come from middle- to upper-middle-class families. They have been given a lot by their parents. In old-fashioned terms, they are spoiled. When it comes to discipline, these parents tend to talk instead of act. They also tend to believe spanking is inappropriate discipline under any circumstances.

- Forty years ago, in even the roughest of schools drawing from the roughest neighborhoods, it was *extremely* rare for a student to threaten a teacher. Today, in even some of the "best" schools drawing from the "best" neighborhoods, teachers have been hit by children as young as ten!

Furthermore, children's violence is directed not just toward other people but also toward themselves. Since 1960, the teen suicide rate has tripled. (The actual increase is probably even higher because researchers note that, as a result of the social stigma associated with suicide, many adolescent suicides—especially when the family is from a small town and is relatively prominent—are classed as accidental deaths.) According to columnist George Will, the suicide rate is rising most rapidly among "younger males (five times more numerous than female suicides) *who are not usually depressed* but are angry, frustrated, resentful, often using drugs and unable to communicate their distress" (emphasis added). Even more telling on the emotional health of America's children is the fact that, for every successful child or adolescent suicide, there are at least fifty to one hundred suicide attempts.

Enough said. This is a book about America's children at risk. The rising tide of child and teen violence is symptomatic of something horribly wrong with our culture, something that has gone wrong over the last forty years. My purpose is to bring that something into the light and help parents protect their children from its ravaging effects.

Part One

The Problem:
What It Is, and What It Isn't

1

Guns: The Red Herring

Thou shalt not kill.

—Exodus 20:13 Authorized (King James) Version (AV)

If it wasn't for Ed Bradley, I might not have written this book. As you probably know, Bradley is an investigative reporter for CBS's *60 Minutes* who does occasional stints as a pundit on other news shows. He's a liberal's liberal, and I don't often agree with him. Nonetheless, I happen to think he's a smart guy who usually constructs an admissible argument.

That's why I was so disappointed in him on the afternoon of April 20, 1999. As what had just happened at Columbine High School was being absorbed by a stunned America, CNN's Larry King asked Bradley why school shootings always occurred in suburban or small town schools.

"Why not inner-city schools?" King asked. "Isn't that where one would most expect such tragedies to happen?"

Without so much as a reflective pause, Bradley proposed that there are more guns in America's suburbs and small towns. "The greater the number of guns in a certain area, the greater the likelihood of such an incident occurring," he said.

Given the ubiquitous problem of unregistered guns (including guns intended for hunting, like shotguns, that many states do not

11

register), there's no way of knowing whether Bradley's premise is correct or not. But I'm going to give him the benefit of doubt. I'll concede that if it was possible to count each and every registered and unregistered gun in America, we'd find that there are indeed more guns per capita in suburban and small-town America than in our inner cities. A *lot* more, probably. This means absolutely nothing.

Consider: A pizza delivery person is far more likely to be shot or robbed at gunpoint in an inner-city neighborhood than in a suburb. More people are killed with guns in America's inner cities than in America's suburbs. More postal workers on the job have been killed by co-workers or former co-workers with guns than employees in any other single business or industry. Bradley would be hard pressed to explain how his "more guns" hypothesis fits any of these facts.

But, let's face it, Bradley had no intention of being objective. What he was disingenuously attempting to do was promote public acceptance of the politically correct notion that school shootings are the result of lax gun control—that they're a Second Amendment problem. I'd love to ask Bradley to please explain why, although most nineteenth-century American children had easy access to family guns that were rarely under lock and key, no record exists of a child in the 1800s going on a shooting rampage in his school or community. Just two generations ago, in many rural areas of the country, teenage boys were allowed to bring guns to school during hunting season! (I attended high school in Valdosta, Georgia, in 1963–64. Our principal was fully aware that many of the boys, including yours truly, had hunting rifles and shotguns in their cars, parked on school property, during hunting season; it was not perceived as even a potential problem.) Not one of those boys ever turned his hunting rifle or shotgun on fellow students and faculty. In fact, such incidents have only taken place in the late-twentieth century, *at a time when gun control laws have been stricter than ever before.*

King's better question would have been, "Why have all these shootings taken place in public schools as opposed to private or church-run schools?" The answer is definitely *not* that upper-middle-class or churchgoing Americans own relatively few guns. Rather, such shootings have never occurred and will probably never occur in an independent school for the simple reason that nonpublic schools are legally able to expel the budding psychopath, something public schools can no longer do. Thanks to the American Civil Liberties Union and other ultraliberal elements in our society, public schools are helpless to do anything about antisocial children but "counsel" them or place them in "alternative" (pseudotherapeutic) programs. Unfortunately, there is no evidence that talking to a psychopath does anything but waste some well-intentioned person's time.

Private and church-operated schools can also provide an education in traditional morality, which presumes that human beings were purposefully created and not the result of a random, accidental, purely physical process. They can tell children that the distinction between right and wrong is not arbitrary but a matter of God's plan for mankind. Once upon a not-so-long-ago time, public schools could do likewise. Then liberals decided that talking about God, even implying His reality, was toxic speech and violated the supposed constitutional mandate of "separation of church and state"—a phrase that is found *nowhere* in the Constitution. In today's public schools, teachers can discuss every conceivable sexual subject even with kindergarten children. But God? Hush!

The same liberal elements mentioned above are responsible for the fact that freedom of speech now includes the "right" of children to express disaffection and disrespect by parading down the halls of a taxpayer-funded school wearing a black trench coat adorned with a swastika and an armband proclaiming I HATE PEOPLE. This is the uniform members of Columbine High School's notorious Trenchcoat Mafia wore to school, day after day, and the school's administration did nothing about it, probably for fear of a lawsuit. In September 1999, I spoke to a group of community leaders in Littleton. I was told by several reputable sources that on the first day of school, not even four months after the shooting, members of the Trenchcoat Mafia wore (under outer clothing) T-shirts proclaiming, in bold print, 13 TO 2: WE'RE WINNING AND IT'S NOT OVER! They took obvious glee in flashing this nefarious message to certain other students during the day. When informed, the school's administration refused to do anything about it, giving the excuse that because the shirts were covered by other clothes, it was not a matter that lay within the school's jurisdiction. The administration was actually saying that if they tried to do something about it, they would raise the likelihood of a lawsuit.

Mental health professionals have aided and abetted the secular left by devising a bogus self-esteem culture that has turned public schools and many homes into virtual "no punishment zones," where children learn that adults do essentially nothing about misbehavior except talk. By Grandma's standards, many of today's children are getting away with figurative murder long before adolescence, courtesy of parents and teachers who have digested thirty-plus years of professional psychobabble to the effect that punishment causes shame, thereby damaging self-esteem. Meanwhile, we have yet to find a better way of dealing with misbehavior than to punish it.

No, even if there are more guns in suburban and small-town America, that's not why little monsters in Littleton, Paducah, Pearl, Springfield, and Jonesboro turned guns on other students, teachers, and themselves. Furthermore, these horrors are not the real issue. They are, again, the tip of the iceberg. The real issue, the one we all need to come to grips with fast, is that America's children have been escalating slowly but surely out of control since the 1960s. In the halcyon days of my adolescence, teens—especially males—were mischievous. Today, teens have become downright dangerous, to themselves and to others. Teen crime in general has risen dramatically over the past thirty years, but most chilling is the fact that children are now committing crimes once associated exclusively with hardened criminals and the criminally insane.

No, the recent tragedy in Littleton is not symptomatic of lax gun control but rather lax parents, lax schools, lax discipline, lax standards, lax expectations, and a culture that has become lax to the point of virtual indifference when it comes to morals, personal responsibility, and critical thinking.

Please don't misunderstand me. I am in favor of reasonable gun control, especially when it comes to allowing children access to guns. I don't think just anyone should be allowed to operate a car, and I don't think just anyone should be allowed to own a gun. But stricter gun control is not going to solve the problem of children who are either bent on hurting other people (child psychopaths) or children who fly impulsively into aggressive rages when they don't get their way (undersocialized, underdisciplined brats).

New laws will not solve the problem. Only parents can. Will they? Will *you*?

2

Human Nature

*And it came about when they were in
the field, that Cain rose up against
Abel his brother and killed him.*

—Genesis 4:8 NJB

Do HUMAN BEINGS, especially males, possess a gene that programs us to be violent in certain situations, in response to certain environmental triggers? Is this gene more powerful than any civilizing influence? Is it going to express itself in one way or another?

There are respectable scientists who believe the answer to all three questions is an unequivocal yes. And then there are respectable scientists who believe in the "violent gene" theory but mitigate it. In their view, the violent gene is stronger, more dominant, more influential in some people than in others. Some posit that this theoretical gene is activated by certain environmental circumstances, such as growing up with abusive parents. In any case, nothing short of identifying the gene in question and removing or altering it during the early years of every human being on the planet through at least four successive generations is going to liberate Homo sapiens from its bloodthirsty thrall. Some experts avoid the mention of the controversial word *gene* altogether and simply say, as does Kellerman in *Savage Spawn,* that violent tendencies seem partly related to certain unnamed biological factors. The fact that these factors cannot be specified means that all this is nothing but speculation, bio-hype.

Whether gene or nebulous biology, we're talking about human *nature* as opposed to *nurture*. But there are actually two entirely different points of view concerning the concept of human nature: one biological, the other spiritual. The modern Darwinian view includes any biological influence—an excess of testosterone, too much serotonin in the brain (or a corresponding lack of the chemical that absorbs serotonin), a gene or genes—that individuals are born with or to which their genotype disposes them. In the modern view, to talk validly about human nature requires biological evidence. By contrast, in the pre-modern (old-fashioned) view, biological evidence is moot. (I use the present tense in the preceding sentence because the pre-modern view is still held by some people, including myself. We are, from a modernist's viewpoint, hopelessly benighted throwbacks.) In the pre-modern view, human nature is a spiritual issue. By virtue of being human, we are all afflicted with a deficiency of spirit. This human spiritual deficiency is independent of biology (nature) and upbringing (nurture). It is simply there, as it was there at the moment of our creation. This deficiency inclines us to sinful or, if you prefer a term with no religious connotation, antisocial behavior.

I have three grandsons, who are five years, two and one half years, and five months old. The two oldest, Jack and Patrick, live two doors away from Willie and me in Gastonia, North Carolina. They are son and daughter-in-law Eric and Nancy's children. Two year-old Patrick is relevant to the present discussion.

But first, a little background: Eric and Nancy are kind, loving, attentive parents. I rate them above average in the discipline department. They tend to employ "peaceful" means of correction, most often sending the children to their rooms for relatively brief periods of time. Both children are reasonably well behaved, very much so when compared to typical children of the same ages. Even Patrick says "thank you" when someone gives him something or does something for him, albeit not without a reminder at times.

Nancy, not without a sense of humor, sometimes describes Patrick as "mean." He is somewhat aggressive, much more so than was his brother at the same age. I attribute some of that to the fact that he's learned how to get what he wants (or hold on to what he already has) notwithstanding competition from his older sibling. Jack is more inclined to use guile to get what he wants. Patrick is more inclined to use brute force, coupled with loud demands. The entire human race should be collectively thankful that Eric and Nancy do not give in to Patrick's totalitarian ways. (I sometimes refer to him facetiously as the "anti-Jack.") But despite his parents' firmness, he is still occasionally "mean."

Shortly after he turned two, Patrick began hitting people, or trying to, when he didn't get his way. More often than not, he aimed for the face. If he was too close to swing with any effectiveness, he'd grab the person's cheeks and squeeze as hard as he could, all the while tensing his body and contorting his features as if he were possessed by some diabolical entity. On one of these occasions, I was the target of his anger. In his rage at something I'd refused to do for him, he dug his fingers so far into the skin of my cheeks that he drew blood!

Where did he learn this? Not from his parents, that's for sure. I am confident that neither of them is in the habit of squeezing people's cheeks. Eric and Nancy maintain a peaceful home, Patrick's occasional outbursts of savagery notwithstanding. Not from Jack, either. Patrick's older brother is anything but aggressive and has always been gentle and kind with him. Patrick has been around other toddlers in a Mothers' Morning Out program, but aside from one "biter" who was removed from the group, Patrick hasn't witnessed or been party to any aggression in that setting either. His playmates in the neighborhood are nonviolent. His parents only allow him to watch nonviolent cartoons and children's shows on television. More often than not, they put on a video like *The Bear in the Big Blue House,* which features a dancing, singing bear who is anything but aggressive. The evidence—or lack of it—strongly suggests Patrick's violence was not learned. If his hitting, scratching, and squeezing blood from people's cheeks was not learned, it must be innate, part of his makeup. Since there is no evidence of *nurture* being the culprit, his aggressiveness must be a matter of his *nature.* If it is Patrick's *nature* to be physically aggressive, then, although it is no longer in evidence, it cannot have been exorcised but, rather, suppressed. How?

At this point, I must make a confession. Patrick's hitting and squeezing didn't just pass like a ship in the night. It *was* exorcised. When he was perhaps two years and two months of age, his parents left him and Jack with us for a long weekend. The first morning of their visit, I was on my knees trying to help Patrick get dressed when he became suddenly infuriated over something. He yelled incoherently (it sounded like a war cry from the movie *Braveheart*), and before I could defend myself, he hauled off and smacked me in the face. I immediately reached around him and swatted his bare buttocks. He stiffened up, his eyes and mouth popped wide open, and he began to wail. I pulled him close and held him tight while he let it out, talking to him the whole time.

"Patrick," I said, "I won't let you hit me. Hitting is a no-no, Patrick. You can't hit people. I love you, Patrick, but I'm not going to let you hit me." When he calmed down, I finished helping him dress and the rest of the day was spent peaceably.

Patrick hasn't hit anyone since, and the abrupt termination of his frequent hitting rules out coincidence. My swift swat to his rear formed a powerful and memorable association with hitting people. Before that, his well-intentioned parents had been trying to talk him out of hitting, or ignoring it, or warding off the hit and saying "no!" Grandpa is from the old school. The point is, Patrick is a smart little guy and he got the message very quickly. More on this in a moment.

Patrick's hitting was by no means atypical of children that age. When frustrated, toddlers often hit, scratch, bite, pull hair, hurl hard objects, and act like brute beasts. Nurture doesn't explain this; the only explanation is nature. A violent gene? Perhaps, but if scientists *never* find such a gene, the evidence will continue to weigh strongly in favor of the idea that aggressiveness is part of human nature—our original, self-centered, instant-gratification-oriented, uncivilized selves.

Let's not forget the third story in the Bible. The first (Genesis 1 and 2) is about creation; the second (Genesis 3) is about, among other things, disobedience; the third concerns aggression. You may recall that Cain becomes "angry and downcast" because "Yahweh looked with favor on Abel and his offering. But he did not look with favor on Cain and his offering." (Genesis 4: 4–5 NJB).

God admonishes Cain for his jealous reaction, telling him, "Sin is crouching at the door hungry to get you. You can still master him" (verse 7b).

God's message couldn't be clearer. Envy, one of the seven deadly sins, is about to consume Cain and drive him to do something violent. But God adds a caveat. Although he is hovering on the brink of disaster, Cain can still *master* his envy. He can bring it under control. Therefore, it's a matter of choice. He is completely responsible for his behavior. The "door" to which God refers is not a physical door, with mass, but the door to Cain's sinful *nature*—a spiritual nature, not a biological one, and therefore amenable to freewill, also known as choice. Sin is crouching at this "door," about to leap through because in his self-centeredness Cain has left the door unguarded. If he doesn't recognize his nature and bring it under conscious control quickly, he will do something horrible. Of course, Cain pays no heed to God's warning. He gives in to his nature, murders his brother, and loses his soul.

Human nature—and here I'm using the term strictly in the spiritual sense—is not a pretty thing. We are by nature self-centered, hedonistic, attracted to sources of instant gratification, greedy, envious, given to laziness, and, yes, prone to aggressive outbursts when we don't get our way. That some scientists believe this nasty nature of ours has genetic roots is really beside the point. Whether or not it is a matter of genes, this nastiness, to one degree or another, is part of every human being from the moment of birth. William Goldman's classic novel *Lord of the Flies* wasn't simply fiction, it was fable. Those innocent little children who turned into murderous, conscienceless savages the minute they were separated from the socializing influence of society were us!

The good news is, our original nature can be "mastered." A child's nature is mastered by parents and other adults who provide proper discipline. The young child, after all, is neither capable of mastering it nor even of recognizing it as something that *needs* to be mastered! To borrow from the vernacular of today's youth, the child is clueless. And be not deceived, it requires a powerful albeit loving discipline to counter the strength of a child's original nature. But parents (and grandparents) can do only so much. The rest is up to the child, who, in maturing, must keep control over what his parents began teaching and then continue learning self-control.

Like every human being ever born, Patrick came into the world with a nature that is partly aggressive. He expressed that particular spiritual deficiency fairly freely until the fateful day when Grandpa persuaded him to "master" it, which Patrick has had no trouble doing since. The mastery of the child's nature, first by adults and then by the child, is what enables civilization—cooperative social orders. The story of my swat to Patrick's rear proves what parents have proved throughout history: human nature is not more power- ful than firm, loving discipline. The question becomes: Are today's children receiving the kind of discipline that ultimately helps them learn to master their not-so-nice natures?

3

Too Little Discipline,
Too Much Talk

Foolishness is bound in the heart of
the child, but the rod of correction
shall drive it far from him.

—Proverbs 22:15 AV

ONCE UPON a not-so-long-ago time, people who subscribed to the Judeo-Christian point of view—which is to say, *most* of Western civilization—believed every child comes into the world carrying a Pandora's box of his or her very own. Contained in this box is pure, unbridled narcissism—the "I deserve what I want, and the ends justify the means" impulse that drives every single antisocial evil. With this went the understanding that adults must keep the lid of the box (the "door," in Genesis 4) closed until the child becomes capable of keeping the lid closed in person.

In the modern era (post-1955), that realistic and pragmatic appraisal was quickly replaced by a romantic one to the effect that every child is an Embodied Being of Holy Light sent to grace us with his or her presence. According to this secular New Age outlook, only the benighted believe every child is capable of evil acts. The New Age view has it that children commit antisocial acts not because of congenital spiritual imperfection, but because of either biological imperfections like bad genes, allergies, or biochemical imbalances, or sociofamilial forces, like the supposedly ubiquitous dysfunctional family. In either case, it is crucial to note that the alleged causative mechanism lies outside the parameters of the child's ability to exercise self-control. The child is not responsible for *any* antisocial act. The modern secular view has it that the child comes into the world spiritually pure, to be subsequently contaminated by either genetic quirks or later sociofamilial "viruses."

The old-fashioned view has it that a child's potential for evil (not the sum total of but *part* of every child's nature) can only be contained with liberal amounts of unconditional love and firm discipline. The child's self-centeredness must be replaced, through firm application of loving discipline, with self-control. The New Age view posits that love is enough, and that the misbehaving child needs not firm discipline but understanding and "help."

Unfortunately for us all, the New Age secular view has prevailed since the late 1960s, even among people who describe themselves as "very religious." It is amazing the number of people I meet who claim strong attachment to Judeo-Christian values and yet are obviously parenting from a secular mind-set. As a consequence, American children have not been properly disciplined for more than a generation. They have been worshiped and treated with kid gloves. Instead of subduing their narcissistic impulse, adults have unleashed it. What today's children want, they think they deserve. And why not? What they want they usually get.

Before the 1960s, "Grandma" (I use the term to refer to our premodern foremothers and forefathers) was the parenting expert. Inexperienced parents who were having a problem with a child weren't likely to seek professional help, even if it had been available. Instead, they'd have gone to Grandma (an elder in their extended families) and asked her advice. Grandma's premise was that these young parents' primary job was that of preparing their children for good citizenship. Everything else—good grades, extracurricular accomplishments—was secondary. Good citizenship was a matter of good character: respect for other people (and especially those in positions of legitimate authority), responsibility, a willingness to admit wrongdoing, honesty, reliability, and the like. The pre-modern family, then, functioned as a workshop for character and citizenship. A child's behavior was viewed as an outward manifestation of his character development, so when a child misbehaved, he was disciplined powerfully to "nip it in the bud." And thus his character development was set back on the right track.

In the 1960s, as America fast became a secular society, parents stopped listening to Grandma, the voice of tradition, and began listening to psychologists and other mental health professionals when it came to rearing children. The new experts emphasized something they called "self-esteem": making children feel wonderful about themselves, making them feel *special*. To promote good self-esteem, the new experts told parents to enter into "democratic" relationships with their children, relationships in which the parties were regarded as equals. Dorothy Briggs, author of *Your Child's Self-Esteem,* one of the biggest parenting sellers of the 1970s, maintained that a child could not learn how to function in a democratic society unless the parent–child relationship was itself democratic. Psychologist and author Thomas Gordon, whom the American Psychological Association eventually honored with a Lifetime Achievement Award, warned that nearly every mental health and social problem could be traced to the traditional exercise of parental authority. In effect, Gordon, Briggs, and other nouveau parenting authorities declared that traditional child-rearing warped the psyches of so many children that all of society was consequently warped.

The new experts said traditional (punitive) discipline, because it makes a child feel bad, was bad for self-esteem. (Note that Grandma thought that when a child did something bad, he *needed* to feel bad about it, and she needed to provide an assist.) Instead of punishing a child when he misbehaves, the new experts said parents should sit down and talk to him to try to discover what is "wrong," what is bothering him. (Note: The child is not wrong; the wrong—which has supposedly caused the misbehavior—lies somewhere else.) The child's feelings, not his behavior, are the primary issue.

This secular view has established a strong foothold in our culture. In his 1999 book *The Men They Will Become,* pediatrician Eli H. Newberger presents what he terms "inductive discipline" as an alternative to punitive forms of discipline. Inductive discipline is the epitome of the nouveau approach, both in terms of method and philosophy. Newberger explains:

> The wrongness is explained in terms of the effect the misbehavior has had on others and/or on the child rather than only in terms of whether an established rule has been broken. Rules are discussed, but they aren't invoked as the beginning and end of the discussion.

As reflected in this passage, Newberger's inductive approach to discipline rests on two presumptions, both of which are secular:

1. *Universal standards of right versus wrong do not exist.* When Newberger states that rules "aren't invoked as the be-

ginning and end of the discussion," he really means human beings are free to set their own standards. This idea was first expressed 2500 years ago by the Greek philosopher Protagoras,
who declared that "man is the measure of all things." That idea
put the human race on the slippery slope.

2. *Children are rational.* They can be reasoned with, talked
into behaving properly.

Both of these ideas hold sway in American culture today. In
fact, it is politically incorrect to think otherwise. To believe truth is
immutable as opposed to being a function of man's capricious-
ness, and to believe children—especially young children—are not
capable of objective reasoning when it comes to their own wants,
desires, and behavior (see Proverbs 22:15, "Foolishness is bound
up in the heart of a child"), is to be hopelessly out-of-date and out
of touch.

Well, consider me hopelessly out of it. I think Newberger not
only is wrong, but his ideas are potentially dangerous. His first
premise, I propose, leads children to believe that something is
wrong only in certain circumstances. Do today's children believe
this? Absolutely! In 1999, syndicated columnist William Raspberry
bemoaned the discovery that more than 80 percent of high school
seniors believed cheating was justifiable in certain circumstances,
such as "I might not have gotten into college otherwise." I propose
that Newberger's second premise leads children to believe they are
little adults; therefore, they only have to obey the rules if they agree
with them (which, paradoxically, is not "adult" by any stretch of
the imagination; it is childish). Do today's children believe this?
Absolutely! Teachers and school administrators all over the country tell me it is not unusual for a child to admit that he or she has

broken a rule, but then say in self-defense that the rule isn't "fair" to begin with.

Newberger's ideas are dangerous because they are anathema to the development of self-control. For a child to learn to control himself, he must first be told in no uncertain terms that standards of right and wrong are fixed, immutable, not matters of circumstance or popular opinion. He must also learn that those standards are not up for discussion or a vote, that what adults in positions of legitimate authority tell him he can, can't, and must do must be obeyed. The father of American education, Noah Webster, said as much in 1836:

> The foundation of all free government and all social order must be laid in families and in the discipline of youth. Young persons must not only be furnished with knowledge, but they must be accustomed to subordination and subjected to the authority and influence of good principles. It will avail little that youths are made to understand truth and correct principles, unless they are accustomed to submit to be governed by them.

Truer words were never written! A child must learn to obey legitimate authority before he can learn self-control. The new parenting experts would say I'm advocating mindless submission to authority, a style of parenting that prevents children from learning to think for themselves. Hogwash! I'll wager my life's savings and all my worldly goods that America's Founding Fathers—Washington, Jefferson, Madison, Franklin, Paine, and so on—were all, as children, told by their parents that right and wrong were immutable and that it was right to obey legitimate authority. Nonetheless, each and every one of these great men grew up thinking for himself, as evidenced by the fact that as adults they took action against what they felt was an illegitimate authority!

Furthermore, I propose that for adults to teach a child to obey legitimate authority is essential to the child's happiness. I have yet to find anyone who will disagree with the following statement: *Where one finds a truly happy child, one also finds an obedient child.* A few sentences ago I said Newberger's ideas (representative of the secular mind-set) were dangerous. Can you imagine anyone more dangerous to society (or himself) than an unhappy person who lacks self-control? That describes every violent person who has ever lived, from Cain all the way down through history to the monstrously evil children who killed twelve classmates and a teacher at Columbine High School and seriously wounded twenty-three others.

Newberger illustrates how to use the inductive method with a boy who's just hit his baby brother because the baby wouldn't share his toys. The mother says, "I know it's hard to share Mommy's attention," and, "I know you are angry when Ben refuses to share his toys." Then, "But you may not hit the baby because it hurts him and it hurts me too. . . . Would you like to build a tower of blocks with me?"

Newberger's inductive approach to discipline is actually nothing more than a rehash of the talking approach described by Thomas Gordon in *Parent Effectiveness Training.* It's well-intentioned, for sure. It "respects" the child's feelings as well as the child's intellect. It is indeed patient. But does it work?

I am absolutely convinced it has not, does not, and will not work. In the first place, I cannot imagine a "discipline" more absurd than offering to play with a boy who's just hurt his baby brother. The older brother pays no price for having hurt someone else. He simply hears an explanation and then gets to play with his mother. I suggest he will continue this aggressive behavior toward his sibling. I further suggest that his aggression will become more and more blatant and he will become increasingly disobedient in a host of other ways as well.

Unfortunately, Newberger's take on discipline is mainstream in the professional community. Take William and Martha Sears, authors of the best-selling *The Discipline Book* and advocates of what is known as "attachment parenting," which amounts to putting the child at the center of attention and keeping him or her there indefinitely. In 1999 on their Web site the Searses answered a question from parents of a four year-old daughter. The parents described the girl as "nasty to us" and said she "even strikes us occasionally and always hits the pets." They set forth a litany of nearly constant misbehavior: cursing, violent temper tantrums, belligerence, disobedience, and destruction, especially when attempts were made to discipline her.

This child was already in serious trouble. Her behavior was highly antisocial, and she was not yet five! The fact that the parents were asking for guidance from "experts" who do not advocate powerful discipline (I do not necessarily mean corporal punishment) suggested their discipline had been lacking all along. My experience tells me the only effective course of action is for the parents to mend their ways and begin employing discipline that will, in Noah Webster's words, cause her to "submit to be governed." I'm talking about a lovingly powerful and consistent exercise of parental authority.

The Searses did not agree with the solution I propose, which would entail a no-tolerance approach to her misbehavior (I'll be more specific about this in chapter 15). They told these parents that their daughter was "angry" and they needed to discover the source of her anger. They suggested it might be her diet or her day-care situation. The parents should begin rewarding her for good behavior either by putting stickers on a chart or by letting her put a coin in a jar every time she cooperated. "Reward charts" say the Searses, ". . . can get an angry child back on track." Angry? This child isn't angry; this child is completely out of control! At age four, she is a menace!

Like so many contemporary child-rearing "experts," the Searses recommend a nonpunitive approach. First, the parents should try to understand why the child is misbehaving. After all, she is simply expressing some dissatisfaction with her life. There's a "reason" for her disobedience, tantrums, cursing, and hitting, and the parents are enjoined to discover the reason and eliminate it from her life. In addition, they are to reward her every time she behaves properly.

In effect, the Searses say this little girl is actually a good child. Her behavior is bad because there is something bad in her life—her diet, perhaps. Through her cursing and hitting, she is simply express-ing—the only way she knows how—that something is bothering her. She cannot "master" what is wrong in her life (change her diet on her own); therefore she is not responsible for her behavior. The parents are responsible for finding the "badness" (they allowed it into her life, after all!) and mastering it for her. In effect, her lack of self-control is excusable. Her fundamental "goodness" must be nurtured, coaxed out of hiding, by rewarding it when it happens.

By contrast, the traditional view would hold that this child has never been taught to master her original nature, which is anything but good. As a consequence, her narcissism has been allowed to spiral out of control and consume her. Her parents, like all parents, are responsible for teaching her to control the impulsive, self-centered expressions of her innate spiritual deficiency. At this point, the teaching will have to be firm and powerful enough to cause this utterly out-of-control child to submit to their authority. Indeed, as Noah Webster put it in 1836, the parents must teach "correct principles" (that is, explain what the rules are, why they are necessary, and why they must punish her when she misbehaves), but the bottom line is her "submission." It is in the child's best interest, as well as the best interest of society, that she learn to obey legitimate authority.

Here we have two examples of violent behavior on the part of children—the first directed toward a defenseless infant, the second toward parents—and in both cases the recommended approach is nonpunitive. In neither case are parents advised to master the child's violent outbursts, so in neither case will the child in question learn to master them.

Remember, this is the same-old same-old stuff the new experts have been recommending for forty years. Forty years is enough time to determine whether this sort of disciplinary approach works or not. I offer the following three "proofs" that it does not work and never will.

1. In 1997, I put the following question to an audience of some five hundred people in Davidson, North Carolina: "How many of you can say with conviction that your children are as well behaved as you were as a child?" I often poll my audiences on various issues, but as this particular query was a first-timer I didn't know exactly what to expect. I guessed, however, that only a hundred hands would go up, thus helping me make the

point that nouveau (child-centered, sentimental, "feel good about yourself") child-rearing doesn't get the same results that the much-demonized traditional child-rearing did. Lo and behold, not one hand went in the air! I've conducted this same poll with more than two hundred audiences since. Never have more than a few hands gone up, even in audiences approaching a thousand people!

2. People who did most of their child rearing prior to 1960 consistently tell me that fifty years ago it was "unheard of" (the phrase they most often use) for a child of three to still be throwing tantrums or openly defying parental authority. Children were mischievous, as they always have been. They often did what their parents had told them not to do when their parents' backs were turned. (I call this the "Adam and Eve syndrome.") But by age three, tantrums and open defiance had stopped. As anyone who's ventured outside their own home in the last ten years knows, the defiant, tantrum-throwing child is everywhere today, and they are not just toddlers but children of all ages. Today, the tantrums and defiance never stop; toddlerhood never ends.

Two recent examples:

a. In an airport recently I witnessed a young girl about age five screaming at her mother to pay attention to her as the mother tried to talk to a ticket agent.

b. Again in an airport: I was standing in the ticket line when I heard a disturbance behind me. Turning around, I saw a father on his knees in front of a little boy around four years old. The child was pummeling his father with his fists as the father tried coaxing him to stop, saying things like, "Now, Brian, you know what we've told you about hitting. Do you need to go outside and calm down? Brian? Please stop and talk to me. We can talk about this, Brian, you don't need to hit." (I thought, Mister, you've talked about this sort of thing entirely too much already. It's time for you to act!)

3. Since 1965, every marker of positive mental health in children has been in a state of decline. No, make that *precipitous* decline. Compared to children of thirty-five years ago, today's kids are more aggressive, more likely to be arrested, and more promiscuous; they are far more likely to be identified as having behavior problems in school and to do less well academically. Today's kids aren't even as happy as children were a generation ago.

"Oh, c'mon, John!" shouts a heckler out there in Readerland. "You can't prove that! There's no happiness measure!"

Oh, yes, I can, and yes, there is. It's called the rate of childhood and teenage depression. By the most conservative estimate, that rate has increased by a factor of 3 in thirty-five years. By some estimates, it has increased by a factor of 10! Whether the former or the latter, it is impossible to conclude anything other than that today's kids are not as happy as children were a generation ago.

In all three of the foregoing "proofs," the behavior of the last generation of American children to be disciplined in traditional (punitive) ways is being compared to the behavior of the first generation of American children disciplined largely in "modern" (nonpunitive, persuasive) ways. Quite simply, there is no evidence that "inductive discipline" works, and every bit of evidence that it *doesn't* work and never will.

Ah! But nouveau parenting experts would have us believe that the relative good behavior of yesterday's child was obtained at great cost to the child's psychological well-being. Was it? I've asked a number of audiences (remember, most of the folks in my audiences represent the last generation of American children reared with powerful discipline), "Raise a hand if you think you were a reasonably well-behaved child." Typically, more than three-fourths of the attendees respond affirmatively. Then, "Keep your hand in the air if you feel you had a happy childhood." Very, very few hands go down. Either the affirmatives are telling the truth or they need memory-recovery therapy. I suspect the former.

Given that my audiences are not a cross-section of American parents but a cross-section of *hard-working, conscientious, well-intentioned* American parents, it's obvious that hard work and good intentions do not a well-behaved child make. What does? I offer my answer in two parts.

1. *A nonintellectual (nonpsychological) approach to child-rearing, one that values good behavior above a child's feelings.* Not that a child's feelings are unimportant, mind you, but parents not so long ago seemed to grasp the fact that sometimes one *must* make a child feel bad (temporarily) in order to promote the general good, not to mention the child's own well-being. Given that most of yesterday's well-behaved kids, at least the ones who come to hear me speak, claim to have had happy childhoods, the psychological consequences of this philosophy were obviously not detrimental. To be more specific, I was reared by parents (a mother and stepfather) who were traditional in their approach to discipline. I did not always like the

manner in which I was disciplined. In fact, they sometimes disciplined me in ways I never used with my own children and would never recommend. But I was not harmed psychologically. Their discipline turned me into a responsible human being. I am anything but an unhappy person. In fact, although I've had moments of unhappiness in my life, I've never been depressed, much less unhappy, for any significant length of time. My marriage has been eminently successful, and our children are doing well in their careers and their own marriages. So much for the idea that traditional discipline is somehow damaging to a child's psyche.

2. *The understanding that children are not angelic beings sent down to grace us with their heavenly presence, but—in Judeo-Christian terms—"sinful" and therefore capable of outrageous behavior.* Until a child is capable of restraining his or her own capacity for outrage, adults must perform this function, or at least teach the child that outrage is not free.

American parents have lost a grip on these commonsensical ideas, all because we let our collective attention, when it came to child-rearing, be turned from the issue of character to the spurious issue of self-esteem—making children feel special. And we allowed ourselves to be swayed by the false notion that Grandma's discipline was psychologically damaging. But why shouldn't we have believed all this nonsense? After all, the people proffering it had capital letters after their names.

4

Feeling Good,
Acting Bad

The sacrifices of God are a broken spirit:
a broken and a contrite heart.

—Psalm 51:17 AV

I WAS ABOUT TO SPEAK in an elementary school in Alabama when my biological nature called. Upon walking into the boys' rest room (no men on the faculty means no men's rest room), I couldn't help but notice a computer-generated banner above the mirror on which was printed, in ten-inch hand-colored letters:

> **You are looking at one of the most special**
> **people in the whole wide world!**

I knew the special person in question wasn't me, so I assumed this is what the school's principal and teachers wanted each and every boy in school to believe. I further assumed this same banner adorned the mirror in the girls' rest room.

It is, of course, a bald-faced lie. The truth is, no one is special. By virtue of being human, one is faulted: in theological (politically incorrect) terminology, sinful. Good parenting—a balance of unconditional love and firm unconditional discipline—equips a child with a sense of social obligation (respect for others) strong enough to successfully suppress his or her narcissistic impulses. The child slowly develops self-respect as a consequence of parents who guide him into respecting other people, not by telling him he's special.

"But John," someone recently rejoined, "I think the idea we should tell children they're special is a reaction to the fact that parents of previous generations didn't think their children were special, much less tell 'em."

That is most definitely *not* a fact. Grandma and Grandpa loved their children and certainly felt each and every one of them was special. But Grandma and Grandpa wisely did not want one of their children to *think* he or she was special, a cut above the rest of humanity.

Steeped as they probably were in the Judeo-Christian understanding of sin and virtue, Grandma and Grandpa valued humility. They knew that pride is authentic only when the person in question is fundamentally humble. Authentic pride, furthermore, is directed *not* at the self but at specific accomplishments. Grandma and Grandpa knew that false pride, the delusion that one's *self* is special, invariably leads to antisocial behavior because the prideful (vain) person feels above reproach and is able to rationalize antisocial outbursts. Remember that pride is one of the seven deadly sins.

The notion reflected on that washroom banner is contrary to a child's best interests. I ask you to consider: Would you be inclined to become friends with someone who clearly thinks he or she is "one of the most special people in the whole wide world"? Of course not! A person who believes that is socially repulsive. Why then are adults in America encouraging children to believe something socially obnoxious about themselves?

Beginning in the 1960s, professional parenting "experts" began telling parents to direct their energies toward nurturing something they called "self-esteem." I've been a critic of this whole idea for most of the twenty-two years I've been writing my nationally syndicated newspaper column. Invariably, when I deal with the subject, someone writes back suggesting that I misunderstand what self-esteem is all about. True self-esteem is a feeling of self-worth based on accomplishments, they point out—what I would call *authentic pride*. I understand the argument they're making, but it turns on itself. If it's not the *self* we're talking about but the good things the self does, then let's not call it *self*-esteem. And while we're at it, let's get rid of the word *esteem* as well. Esteem means worship, and if self-worship is really not what the secularists have in mind (I happen to think it is *exactly* what they have in mind!), let's call it something else. Hey! We don't have to invent a new term here. *Responsible* will more than suffice.

The world would be a better, steadily improving place if adults concentrated on simply teaching children to be responsible: to have compassion and respect for others (social responsibility), to do their best (task responsibility), and to do the right thing even when no one else is watching (personal responsibility).

Above all else, I suggest we need to bring an emphasis on teaching humility back into the child-rearing equation. There is no one more obnoxious than someone who thinks he's special, and no one more charming than a person who's more interested in you than in telling you about himself.

I encourage the well-intentioned principal of that Alabama elementary school to tear down the YOU'RE SPECIAL banners and replace them with banners that read, DO SOMETHING SPECIAL FOR SOMEONE ELSE TODAY.

The term *self-esteem* has caused untold damage to our culture. Recent research supports my position. Consider:

- In a recent international academic competition, American high school students came in dead last. They tended to believe, however, that they'd done really well. Korean students, who ranked near the top, were inclined to believe they hadn't done very well at all. It's beginning to look as if good self-esteem may be more of a hindrance than a help to actual achievement. It also looks as if feeling really good about oneself lends itself to delusional thinking about one's performance on tasks. It also looks as if humility (still a value in Asia) lends itself to higher achievement.
- After studying high self-esteem in children, two psychologists recently concluded that children with inflated feelings of worth that are unsupported by real accomplishment are prone, when their precarious self-image is threatened, to become aggressive and even violent.
- Lending support to this study, researchers have found that violent criminals doing hard time in maximum-security prisons were likely to score significantly higher on a measure of self-esteem than the average law-abiding citizen.

That last finding is especially surprising considering psychologists have steadfastly maintained that it is *low* self-esteem that causes violence and aggression, along with a host of other social pathologies. The latest evidence, however, supports the exact opposite view! In 1996, researchers at Case Western Reserve University and the University of Virginia conducted a large-scale study of the relationship between self-esteem and violent behavior. Here's a sampling of their startling conclusions:

- Aggressors seem to believe that they are superior, capable beings. Signs of low self-esteem, such as self-depreciation, humility, modesty, and self-effacing mannerisms, seem to be rare among violent criminals and other aggressors.
- Gang members apparently think, talk, and act like people with high self-esteem, and there is little to support the view that they are humble or self-deprecating or even that they are privately full of insecurities and self-doubts.
- Violent youths seem sincerely to believe that they are better than other people.
- Violence is most common when favorable self-appraisals are threatened (causing self-doubt) ... violence is a means of evading such doubts and affirming the favorable views of self.

Isn't that interesting! Or perhaps *Isn't that scary?* is the better question. A generation or so ago, the experts began telling parents that high self-esteem would lead to better grades and better behavior, and prevent drug and alcohol use. Unfortunately, it hasn't turned out that way. In fact, the whole notion of building good self-esteem in children seems to have backfired big-time. What the researchers clearly discovered is that people who are humble and modest are not likely ever to become violent. Is this not biblical? Is not pride one of the seven "deadly" sins? Just goes to prove there is nothing new under the sun—except perhaps the children's liberation movement. Yes, there is a movement afoot in America, supported by a number of leading legal and political figures, to liberate children. From what? Why, from traditional childhood, what else?

Harvard law professor Laurence Tribe has proposed, for example, that childhood be considered a "semisuspect" classifica-
tion, meaning that its implications are capitalized upon by parents
and schools to maintain children in a state of mindless servility. In
the mid-1970s, Hillary Rodham Clinton published a series of law
articles, later reprinted in the *Harvard Law Review,* arguing for the
extension of legal rights for children. The "rights" in question
would allow them to bypass parental permission when it comes to
abortion, parenthood, cosmetic surgery, treatment of venereal dis-
ease, and employment!

Kay Hymowitz is a senior fellow at the Manhattan Institute
and author of *Ready or Not: Why Treating Children as Small Adults
Endangers Their Future—And Ours.* In her book, Hymowitz argues
that child liberation ideas entered the mainstream in the 1960s and
evolved into what she terms "anticulturalism"—the nefarious
notion that socializing the young to certain values is a wrongful
attempt on the part of the strong to manipulate the weak and
defenseless. Anticulturalists believe children should be allowed to
develop independently of a priori assumptions concerning right
versus wrong. Children will make good decisions for themselves,
the argument goes, and need to be allowed the freedom to do so.
Eli Newberger, author of *The Men They Will Become,* is an anticul-
turalist, as is Thomas Gordon, author of *Parent Effectiveness
Training* (see Chapter 3).

Anticulturalism has become the dominant ideology of the
mental-health, child-development, and education professions.
Columnist John Leo, another voice in the secular wilderness, writes:

It boils down to the notion that children should be allowed
to develop on their own; that parents and schools should

stimulate and encourage but otherwise stay out of the way. The emergence of the moral self must not be quashed by what Harvard psychologist Carol Gilligan calls the "foreign voice-overs of adults." Children are not to be raised, but simply allowed to grow.

This ideology is called anticulturalism for good reason. It is antithetical to the essence of every viable culture: a stable core of values passed from one generation to the next.

In schools, anticulturalism expresses itself in "open classrooms," "values clarification," "cooperative learning," "whole language," "outcome-based education," and nearly every other fad that's been paraded down the halls of American public education over the past forty years. A study by the Public Agenda research group revealed that only 7 percent of education professors think a teacher's primary job is to convey knowledge while 92 percent believe teachers should simply "enable students to learn on their own." This is the concept of the teacher as facilitator of a feely-good "self-discovery" group. Says syndicated columnist Mona Charen, mincing no words:

> Keen to instill self-esteem but contemptuous of mere facts, our schools have turned out ignoramuses by the millions. And, an ironic fillip, these products of anticultural education are more bored and less in love with education for its own sake . . . than their predecessors, who survived old-fashioned instruction.

Anticulturalism expresses itself in the mental-health professions in family therapy, where the feelings and opinions of the child or children are often accorded more validity than the parent's values. Psychologist and author Thomas Gordon asserts that children should be treated as adults *because that's the way they want to be treated*. The idea that children are exploited by parents and the adult community in general was at the rotten core of "recovered memory therapy," the nefarious practitioners of which assumed that nearly all adult emotional problems were the result of repressed memories of childhood sexual abuse, usually by one's father.

Among child-development specialists, anticulturalism has taken the form of advice from "experts" like pediatrician T. Berry Brazelton to let children toilet-train themselves when they're ready, even if they show no inclination to do so until age four or five! It expresses itself in the "attachment parenting" movement, the gurus of which believe it is more important that children "bond" than that their parents discipline them to certain behavioral standards (see my comments on William and Martha Sears in chapter 3).

Kay Hymowitz hits the head of anticulturalism's nail: "What seems to be sensitivity to children's energy and creativity turns out to be surrender to their restless, excitable natures and to the superficial pleasures they already know so well." Right on!

The aforementioned ideas are not just anticultural, they are antiscriptural as well. The scriptural view asserts that human being are inclined toward self-centered purposes that are usually out of sync with respect for others; the secular view holds that each and every child is naturally good. The good news is that anticulturalism, while still the dominant cultural force in America, and especially on America's college campuses, seems to be on the wane. From all that I gather in my travels, there is a strong cultural recovery movement afoot in these United States, as exemplified by the following:

- An ever-growing number of Americans who do not trust mental health professionals to give good guidance, especially on child-rearing matters.
- Numerous successful lawsuits against the practitioners of recovered-memory therapy.
- The growing demand for competency testing for teachers.
- The turn against social promotion as well as the new emphasis on educational standards.
- The fact that you are reading this very procultural book.

A generation of American parents became convinced that psychologists and other so-called (and often self-proclaimed) experts knew more than the sages about human nature and how to rear children properly, and all of America is now reaping what these mental-health professionals have sown. Perhaps the single most alarming outcome of self-esteem-based parenting with its non-punitive approach to discipline is the nationwide epidemic (and from all I can gather, it is confined to the United States) of children hitting their parents, especially their mothers.

5

Mother-Battering

A wise son makes a father glad,
but a foolish son is a grief to his mother.

—Proverbs 10:1 NJB

Today's women are a paradoxical bunch. They are rightfully proud of the professional and political inroads they've made, yet they all too often tolerate from and do for their children what they will not tolerate from and do for a grown male. The patriarchy has been replaced by the toddler-archy.

My mother (a single parent at the time) made it clear by the time I was four years old that I was capable of entertaining myself, dressing myself, putting myself to bed (albeit she always tucked me in, heard my prayers, and often read me a bedtime story), resolving spats with friends on my own, and fixing myself a snack. She was, in effect, no longer "working" for me (finding things to do for me, coming to my infantile beck and call); rather, I was "working" for her. She told me what to do, and I did it. She tolerated no disobedience, so although I was mischievous I did not openly disobey. I was comforted to learn from my playmates that their mothers were equally commanding. And by the way, I do not remember my mother ever yelling at me to do something or so much as threatening me with a spanking.

Never, ever, would I have taken a swing at my mother. To my knowledge, none of my childhood playmates ever tried to hit their mothers either. Unfortunately, hitting one's mother is no longer unheard of. It is not even uncommon. Over the past few years, dozens upon dozens of mothers have asked me what to do when their children hit them—and they are not referring to toddlers but to children three and older. The mere question, "What should I do about it?" reflects the problem. That adult women are paralyzed by intellectual indecision at such moments is profoundly disturbing.

"What would your mother have done?" I asked a woman who told me she is the target of frequent physical violence from her five-year-old son.

"I don't really know, but the first time I did it would have been the last," she said, without elaborating.

"Would she have physically abused you?"

"Oh, no!" she replied. "But she would have nipped it in the bud."

"Do you realize that the next time your child takes a swing at you can also be the last time?" I asked.

"But *why* is he hitting me?" she asked.

"Because you allow it," I said. "You allow it by trying to understand *why* he's doing it. Now, please stop trying to understand it and *do something about it!*"

"But what?" she pleaded.

"The Fifth Commandment instructs us to honor our mothers and fathers. You would do your mother great honor if you allowed her to be your mentor here."

I can only hope she went home and ended her son's abuse as her mother would have done under similar circumstances. She would do her son, herself, and the rest of us an inestimable favor. But who knows? She may still be trying to understand him and reason with him.

The epidemic of mother-battering is but one of many prices we are currently paying for allowing "helping" professionals to sell us a sentimental, romantic vision of children and child-rearing. Our foremothers and forefathers knew that children, being human, were unworthy of being romanticized. They also knew that misbehavior did not need to be "understood," only punished.

By the time her child was three years old, yesterday's no-nonsense mom had stopped doing what today's "liberated" woman continues doing indefinitely—serving, tolerating, and otherwise enabling narcissism, the infantile "I want it, therefore I deserve it!" impulse that lies behind every antisocial act.

It has long been recognized that the child is father to the man. What is a five-year-old boy who can hit his mother without consequence going to do when he is thirty years old and his wife irritates him? The answer is downright ugly, especially when that five-year-old is but one of thousands like him.

A large part of the problem is that the current crop of children represents the NO FEAR generation. This label came to me one day while driving down the interstate near my home. Suddenly, a car flashed by on my left going at least 30 mph over the speed limit. For an instant, I heard the *thump-thump-thump* of one of those auditory obliterators young people call car stereos and saw the unmistakable profile of a baseball hat turned around backward.

One plus one equals rude, obnoxious teenager. Affixed to the back windshield was a decal that read NO FEAR.

It hit me like a ton of bricks. This present generation of young people is indeed the NO FEAR generation! They appear—with exceptions, of course, but they are not in my estimation the rule—to share a lack of fear bordering on utter disdain where consequences are concerned. Like teens in all times and places, including my school friends and me, today's teens believe they are invincible. Therefore, they do reckless things. But it's more than that. Even if we didn't fear the consequences of driving at breakneck speed, my teenage peers and I nonetheless feared adults and the consequences they stood ready to assign us at a moment's notice when we misbehaved. Not so with today's teens. They have no fear.

And why should they? When I was a boy, if I misbehaved in school my teacher punished me, and when I got home my parents punished me again. Today, if a boy misbehaves in school, he is sent to a counselor who talks. When he gets home, he tells his parents, who just might call the school to protest that his "punishment" was too harsh, that singling him out was "unfair."

These days, when a child misbehaves, adults might bluster about what they're going to do if he does it again. He does it again, and again adults bluster about what they're going to do if he does it again. And so it goes.

Thirty-five years ago, my teenage co-conspirators and I took pains to be sure adults wouldn't discover our transgressions. Today's teens, from all accounts, don't seem to care if adults find out about the bad things they do. Why should they? We've given them no reason to believe anything of real consequence is going to happen.

In recent public presentations, I've been pointing out that, as children, baby boomers were afraid of their parents. But today's parents—in most cases, grown-up baby boomers—are afraid of their children. They're afraid their children will misbehave in public. They're afraid their children will think they are not sufficiently loved. They're afraid their children will become upset with them. But most of all, they're afraid their children will not like them.

When I was a child, I was very, very wary of misbehaving in public. Even if my mother or stepfather wasn't there, I was afraid they might find out. If I had yelled "You don't love me!" at my mother, she would have ignored it, and I would have been afraid of what might be coming next. I would get upset at my parents, but I was careful to hide it, for fear of the consequences. And, by the way, my mother never spanked me, and my stepfather spanked me a total of perhaps five times between ages seven and twelve, after which I cannot remember a spanking. Furthermore, my parents didn't give a hoot whether or not I approved of them at any given moment.

My parents were by no means unique in this regard. And yet, except during moments of childish self-pity, I never doubted that they loved me.

I asked a recent audience, "How many of you were afraid of your parents?"

I'd say one out of every two attendees raised a hand. I followed up with, "Please keep your hand up if you knew, in your more rational moments, that your parents loved you heart and soul."

No more than a few hands went down, illustrating that fearing one's parents and knowing they love you are by no means incompatible.

Am I suggesting it is right and proper for children to fear their parents? Yes, but I'm not referring to a lose-control-of-your-bladder-when-your-parents-walk-into-the-room sort of fear. Rather, I mean fear in the biblical sense.

As Jerry Bridges, the author of *The Joy of Fearing God*, reminds us, the Old Testament proclaims that "there is joy in fearing the Lord." In this ancient context, *fear* is synonymous with wonder, reverence, and an admiring esteem for God's omnipotence, along with the knowledge that this awesome power is the very power of love, a love so strong that it commands *obligation*. That's what a healthy fear of God is all about, and that is also what a healthy fear of one's parents is all about.

That, too, is part of the problem. Today's children don't seem to feel a strong sense of obligation to their parents. And who can blame them? After all, today's parents act as if the only people with obligation in the parent-child relationship are parents. Today's typical child is wanting not only in the desire to please but also in a strong desire not to disappoint. It's the parents who are supposed to do the pleasing and who are often downright afraid of not being pleasing enough.

Someone recently suggested to me that this was nothing more than the product of a perpetually swinging "parenting" pendulum. Wait a few years, she said, and the pendulum will begin to swing back. I think not. If this is a swinging pendulum, where is the evidence it has ever swung before? This is more like something turned upside down, and things turned upside down do not right themselves like pendulums that eventually must swing in the other direction. They must be righted. Parents can start by helping children discover the joy of fearing them and come to the realization that their awe-inspiring power is, in fact, the power of love.

That will put an end to the mother-battering epidemic, and none too soon.

6

Toddlerhood ad Nauseam

There is a generation that curses their
father and does not bless their mother.

There is a generation that are pure in their own
eyes and yet is not washed from their filthiness.

There is a generation, Oh, how lofty are their
eyes! and their eyelids are lifted up.

—Proverbs 30:11–13 NJB

Hıstorically, tantrums, hitting, and open defiance of adult authority ("No! I won't!") are associated with toddlerhood, and toddlerhood only. Before to the modern era, which began around
1955 when television became a staple in the American household,
toddlerhood was over by age three. By the mid-1970s, toddlerhood
had become never-ending. Today, many children never stop throwing tantrums, and they never stop defying authority—openly, even
belligerently. The toddler has a short attention span, is impulsive,
doesn't stay focused on anything for long, and is typically hyperactive. The list of problem behaviors associated with Attention
Deficit Hyperactivity Disorder as published in the latest edition of
the *Diagnostic and Statistical Manual* is perfectly descriptive of a
typical toddler. Today, many older children never develop long

attention spans, never stop being impulsive, unfocused, hyperactive. It's not unusual for a frustrated toddler to hit a parent, but a good number of older children never stop hitting their parents, their mothers especially. Before 1955, it was highly unusual to find a twenty-four-month-old child who was still wearing diapers. Today, it's not unusual to find a child of three, or even four years old, still wearing diapers. In 1999, disposable diaper manufacturers came out with sizes for children as old as six! (I call them Little Depends.)

The toddler is the perfect picture of narcissism. He wants to be first, he wants the biggest, and he believes he deserves what he wants. He demands instant gratification. He wants to be served and becomes angry if he is not served quickly and properly.

In short, the toddler is a mirror of human nature—aggressive, demanding, self-centered, disobedient, petulant, and jealous. His nervous system is immature, resulting in poor impulse control and occasional chaotic activity. He's irresponsible, often destructive, and careless.

I propose that "new" parenting has had the effect of extending toddlerhood indefinitely. With its emphasis on self-esteem, nouveau parenting panders to self-centeredness. Because it embodies the notions that traditional discipline was psychologically abusive and that children can be talked into behaving properly, it panders to misbehavior. Because today's typical parents expose children to electronic media during the most critical phase of brain development—the preschool years—many children never develop adequate attention spans. Because today's typical parents don't require their children to perform chores around the house from age three on, strictly as a service to the family, today's children wallow in infantile irresponsibility long past the time Grandma used to cure it.

Grandma cured her child's toddlerhood by the time he was three—in other words, on schedule. By his third birthday, Grandma's child was paying attention to her. He was doing what she told him to do. He was no longer stomping his feet and screaming when he didn't get his way. Between his second and third birthdays, Grandma had brought about a revolution in his life, one that altered their relationship forever.

During the first two years, Grandma orbited around her child in a constant ministry of service. As she bathed and fed and changed and carried and soothed and rocked her baby to sleep, he became convinced that Grandma was his personal servant for life. By the time he was two, he was absolutely certain that he was the center of Grandma's universe.

Grandma knew this first stage of the parent-child relationship had to come to a relatively early end, lest she raise a thoroughly obnoxious narcissist—otherwise known as a spoiled brat. So Grandma began bringing the curtain down on phase one of parenthood—the servanthood phase—when her child was between eighteen and twenty-four months of age. One of the first things she undertook to stop being a servant was toilet training. In 1960, 95 percent of twenty-four-month-old children had been successfully toilet-trained. Grandma knew that as long as she was laying her child down several times a day, wiping, powdering, and putting on dry diapers, he would perceive her as a servant. It is significant to note that many supposed "experts," most notably pediatrician and author T. Berry Brazelton, tell parents it's perfectly all right not to toilet-train until a child is as old as four or five. This does nothing but extend the mother's servanthood, indefinitely if not forever. It sets the stage for numerous ongoing problems, the least of which is resistance to being toilet-trained.

Between the second and third birthdays, Grandma upset the status quo. She took her child out of the center of *her* attention and placed herself at the center of *his* attention. She did this by beginning to communicate instructions in no uncertain terms, and staying the course through protests and defiance. She may have popped his bottom—now no longer padded by diapers—when he stood his ground and refused to obey. She refused to do things for him that he could do for himself. She ignored his tantrums or put him in his room when he threw one, letting it run its course. She did not function as his playmate, but insisted that he find things to do and stay out from under foot. And for all these reasons, by the time he was three, he saw his mother through new eyes. She now loomed large in his life. Once a servant, she was now an imposing authority figure, and *he* was paying attention to *her*.

Having secured his awe and attention, she wasted no time in putting him to work for her. I was raised by a mom who represents the last generation of Grandmas—sturdy female parents who took control of the parent-child relationship early in its development. By the time I was four, I was washing floors. I don't remember how that came about; I can only imagine that one day my mother approached me and simply said, "I have a lot to do today and I need your help. I'm going to teach you how to wash a floor. Come with me."

And that was that. Ten minutes later, I was washing my first floor. By the time I was five, my mother had taught me to wash my own clothes in her "washer," a galvanized tub with hand rollers bolted to it. Again, I don't remember how the first time came about, but I imagine something along these lines: "I washed those pants yesterday, and you've gotten them dirty already. I'm not going to wash your clothes every day. Besides, you're old enough to learn to wash 'em yourself. Come with me. I'll show you how."

Once again, that was that. My mother didn't mince words when it came to giving me instructions. She didn't cajole, bribe, promise a reward, or try in any other fashion to persuade me to obey. She just told me the way it was going to be. When I misbehaved, she told me how disappointed I had made her and sent me to my room for a prolonged period of private contemplation.

She never would have spoken to me the way today's parents speak to their kids: "Hey! I've got an idea! How would you like to learn to wash floors today? I know! If you'll help me wash this floor, I'll put a star on your chart and you'll be one star closer to getting that new bicycle! How about it?"

Not on your life. There was no negotiating with my mom, no wimpy attempts to entice me to obey her. She came straight to the point, and I obeyed. And as a consequence of her "psychologically incorrect" parenting style, my toddlerhood was over by the time I was three. I'd thrown my last tantrum and said "no!" for the last time to one of her instructions. She served me for two years. By the time I was four, I was serving her. She wiped my bottom for almost two years. By the time I was four, I was washing her floors.

Because my mother ended my toddlerhood by the time I was three, I went to school two years later prepared to *pay attention to women,* prepared to *accept assignment from women,* and prepared to *obey women.* I took women seriously. When a woman said something, I listened. When a woman told me to do something, I did it.

Oh, yes, I was mischievous. I did what I was not supposed to do when adults weren't looking. But I did not, when told to do something, defy, yell, or say things like "You're a dummy!" I said "Yes, ma'am" or "Yes, sir," and that was that. I might not have wanted to do what I was told, but I did it. More often than not, however, I remember taking pride in what I did. It gave me a chance to show adults how capable I was.

The American mom no longer has permission to make the transition from servant to authority figure during her child's third year of life. Today's woman has been led to believe that the "good" mother does as much for her child as she possibly can, is highly involved in his life, pays him the most attention, and fixes it whenever he gets upset—in perpetuity, mind you. If the teacher upsets him, she runs down to the school to fix it. If a playmate upsets him, she bustles outside to fix it. If she can't fix it with the playmate, she hurries down the street to fix it with the playmate's mother. If homework upsets her child, she fixes it. Last but hardly least, if *she* upsets her child, she fixes it.

My mother never thought it was her responsibility to fix any of those things, and in that regard she was typical of the pre-modern mom. She expected me to fight my own battles, lie in the beds I made, and paddle my own canoe. If I complained about a teacher, my mom assumed the teacher was having problems with *me*, not the other way around. If Mom made a decision that upset *me*, she felt my upset showed she had done the right thing.

Today's mom is in a perpetual state of servitude to her children. To demonstrate her commitment to them, to prove her devotion, she runs herself ragged in their service. She never cuts the umbilical cord or unties the apron strings. As a consequence, her children never really grow up. They remain toddlers forever—

petulant, whining, ungrateful, demanding, disrespectful, and disobedient. The more immature they act, the more convinced she
becomes that she's not doing enough for them. And around and
around they all go, in a never-ending dizzy dance of mother-child
codependence.

7

Punishment and, Yes, Even the S-Word

Correct your son, and he will give you comfort; he will also delight your soul.

—Proverbs 29:17 NJB

O<small>N</small> February 14, 1998, an article in *The New York Times Sunday Magazine* declared, "While research has shown that children turn out best in families in which parental demands are enforced, that is true only if the punishment is not punitive." Is this true? No, it is not.

In the first place, punishment is, by definition, punitive. I trust the author meant to say "... that is true only if the *consequences* are not punitive." Even then, the statement is false.

The truth: Some researchers claim to have produced evidence that punishment is counterproductive, but a landmark study that has withstood the test of time affirms otherwise.

In 1971, psychologist Diana Baumrind published the results of her longitudinal study on parenting styles. After twenty-six years and counting, Baumrind's research is considered classic, the best of the best. After comparing styles she termed *authoritarian* (high expectations, low nurture), *authoritative* (high expectations, high nurture), and *permissive* (low expectations, high nurture), Baumrind found that authoritative parents *who tend to employ spanking (in moderation) as well as other punitive consequences* rear the most well-adjusted, well-behaved children. Most interesting was a finding concerning permissive parents, almost all of whom reported they did not believe in spanking. In one-on-one interviews, however, many of these same parents admitted to explosive attacks of physical rage toward their children. Baumrind decided that "they apparently became violent because they could neither control the child's behavior nor tolerate its effect upon themselves."

No reasonable person would argue that the more punishment the better. Punishment can certainly be overused, and any given punishment can be overdone. Furthermore, as I have said in previous books (such as *A Family of Value*), the essence of effective discipline is not punishment, or even the correct selection of consequences, but communication. Discipline is the process of creating a *disciple* out of your child, someone who will follow your lead. It is leadership, not punisher-ship. Good leaders are good communicators; they are adept at bringing out the best in people. This applies to parenting as well as the workplace. Nonetheless, where misbehavior is concerned, Baumrind's research is unequivocal: punitive consequences (taking away privileges, restriction, spanking) not only work better than nonpunitive ones (reasoning, threats) but also are most effective when used as a *first* resort.

I also take issue with the implication contained in the *Times* article that parents should *demand* obedience. They should expect obedience, yes, and they should command it, but a parent who finds him- or herself *demanding* obedience on a fairly routine basis does not know how to command. Again, the essence of good command is good communication. For a parent, this means *acting as if you know what you want your child to do and not do and communi-*

cating your expectations straightforwardly, in no uncertain terms. It also means being willing to punish—and powerfully—when your child willfully disobeys. And speaking of powerful punishment, what about spanking?

Along those lines, I suppose the first question to be answered is, "Do I believe in spanking?"

Answer: No, I don't *believe* in spanking in the sense that it's essential to a proper upbringing. I am absolutely convinced one can rear a child well without ever spanking. Nor do I believe spanking is the defining issue the media make it out to be. There are good parents who spank and good parents who don't, and the same is true of bad parents as well as the vast majority of parents—well-intentioned—who fall somewhere between.

I believe, however, that with certain children who misbehave in certain ways in certain situations, a properly administered spanking is the best parental course of action. The certain misbehaviors in question all fall in the *outrageous* category, such as outrageous defiance, outrageous disobedience, outrageous disrespect, and outrageous tantrums. The certain situations are those where the outrage needs to be stopped quickly, for the good of all concerned. By properly administered I mean a couple of swats applied to the child's rear with the parent's hand. The *certain children* referred to are those who, once they cross the line of outrage, tend to deteriorate rapidly. The swats are delivered simply for the purpose of stopping the snowball of misbehavior before it starts rolling downhill and focusing the child's attention on the parent, whose job then becomes to assign a *more effective consequence.*

You heard that right. A spanking, as I define it, is not discipline. It is a consequence, to be sure, but not all consequences are disciplinary. Discipline is teaching, and a spanking, by itself, teaches nothing. The teaching is done immediately thereafter by a parent who communicates well and follows up on the spanking with a explanation that conveys "correct principles" and a consequence that does indeed convey a lesson.

When my daughter Amy was seven or eight, I popped her rear end once when she screamed at me for assigning a chore to her rather than to her brother ("You always make me do everything!"). Once having brought an abrupt end to her histrionics, I spoke firmly to her about yelling at authority figures and sent her immediately to her room for the rest of the day (after she performed the chore). The lesson? Screaming is antisocial and will result in your being removed from the immediate social situation. She never screamed defiantly at either her mother or me again, not because of being popped on her rear but because she did not like being confined to her room.

I believe most parents who spank do it entirely too often, so often that spankings lose their meaning. I also believe there's something sadistic about a spanking delivered in ritual fashion: requiring the child to go to his or her room and wait a dramatically long period of time for the parent, pull down his or her pants, bend over, and so on. I believe the best spanking is a "bolt out the blue, once in a blue moon"—no threats, no dramatic buildup, but rather a spontaneous happening that's over as quickly as it started.

I do not believe spankings per se are abusive, although like any other consequence they can be so administered. This is not the majority view among mental-health professionals. The majority view was well expressed by a Dayton, Ohio, therapist who wrote a guest editorial published in May 1999 in the *Dayton Daily News.* The headline read, EXPERTS SHOULDN'T PROMOTE SPANKING: ACT

OF VIOLENCE SENDS WRONG MESSAGE TO OUR CHILDREN. Her comments were representative of what America's spanking abolitionists would have the public believe, so they merit examination.

First, she claimed that "spanking gives a child the message that people who love each other hit each other." The child reasons that if parents who love you, hit you, then love and hitting go together. Thus, spankings "train people to accept violence in family relationships." The source of this unscientific rhetoric is the guru of the antispanking movement, Murray Straus, director of the Family Research Center at the University of New Hampshire and author of *Beating the Devil Out of Them*. Dr. Straus's research, which I examined in my previous book *To Spank or Not to Spank*, violates just about every procedural rule possible. Even one of his former graduate assistants, Robert Larzelere, whose own research into spanking is distinguished for its reasoned objectivity, is among the ranks of those critical of Straus's methods. Suffice it to say that Straus has established no reliable connection whatsoever between being spanked as a child and later becoming a spouse-beater or someone prone to violence in any context.

Parenting, the Dayton therapist went on to say, is all about helping children establish self-control. I agree with that. Ah, but she goes on to say spanking is "more likely to breed anger, resentment, and revenge."

Oh really? Remember my swat to my grandson Patrick's rear end when he smacked me in the face. Remember, too, that he has not hit anyone since. Furthermore, he and I have a most affectionate, playful relationship. Where is the evidence of his being angry, resentful, or vengeful toward me? There is none. Nor is there any evidence in the overwhelming majority of children who are spanked by their parents.

My Dayton critic correctly made the point that many parents use spanking as a quick fix. As I say most clearly in *To Spank or Not to Spank,* the problem with spankings is that most parents don't know how to employ them properly. The three most common parental errors in this regard are thinking that spankings will "cure" a behavior problem in and of themselves, failing to follow up on a spanking with a more effective consequence, and spanking so often that the child in question develops an immunity to them.

But the Dayton therapist follows this step in the right direction by revealing the agenda at the heart of the antispanking movement: to wit, the creation of antispanking law. If it's illegal for a husband to hit his wife, she asks, why is it legal for a father to hit his child, someone even more defenseless? Good question! In the first place, it is *by no means* legal for a father to *hit* his child indiscriminately. It is only legal for a parent to *spank,* defined as an open-handed swat to a child's buttocks. And therein lies the rub. By disingenuously equating a punch to a spouse's face with a swat to a child's rear, spanking abolitionists hope to influence lawmakers to enact law that would effectively enable government to dictate to parents how they can and cannot discipline their children. If well-intentioned people like Murray Straus succeed in their crusade, the door to government intervention in child-rearing will crack open. And as history has taught, government is never content with getting just a foot in the door.

That Dayton therapist, well-intentioned as she may be, is in the thrall of antispanking rhetoric. Here are the facts:

Fact : More than four out of five American adults who were spanked by their parents say spanking was an effective form of discipline, and more than two out of four say it was *very* effective.

Fact : Childhood aggressiveness has been more closely linked to maternal permissiveness than to even *abusive* physical punishment.

Fact: There is absolutely no good, scientifically grounded evidence that would suggest spankings per se incline children toward violent behavior. Researchers who claim to have established that connection (such as Murray Straus) have violated almost every rule of scientific evidence-gathering in order to advance what is clearly a personal bias.

Fact: No anecdotal evidence exists to support the idea that spankings cause children to think hitting is okay. Most of the members of my generation were spanked as children, but we baby boomers are not, as a rule, apt to hit others when we're upset.

Fact: Over the last thirty years, the percentage of American parents who spank has decreased. During that same period, however, violent behavior on the part of teenagers (irrespective of socioeconomic status) has increased dramatically. Obviously, it is simplistic to think America would be a more peaceful place if parents didn't spank.

Fact: Psychologist Diana Baumrind's research (summarized earlier) certainly suggests that parental self-control is actually enhanced when the parent gives him- or herself permission to spank.

Fact: Sweden outlawed parental spanking in 1979. Follow-up studies have failed to find that physical abuse of children has declined. In fact, consistent with Baumrind's aforementioned finding, a 1995 study conducted by the Swedish government found a fourfold increase in serious parental abuse of children since the law was enacted.

Fact: In 1996, after a long and protracted battle over the issue of spanking, the American Academy of Pediatrics held a two-day conference on The Short- and Long-term Consequences of Physical Punishment. Twenty-four experts, most of whom were opposed to the use of spanking under any circumstances, were invited to share research and opinions on the subject. After hearing the evidence pro and con, the two co-chairs of the conference, both of whom had come convinced that spanking was always bad, stated that they now believed, based on the evidence, that *"given a relatively 'healthy' family life in a supportive environment, spanking in and of itself is not detrimental to a child or predictive of later problems."*

Fact: Dr. Robert Larzelere, formerly one of Murray Straus's graduate assistants, was one of the conference participants. His review of eighteen scientific studies on spanking, those with the strongest designs and methods, found that spanking produced more beneficial outcomes than any disciplinary alternative.

I am convinced that a child who is secure in his parents' love does not perceive himself as the victim of a "violent" act when spanked by those parents. To such a child, a spanking is a spanking, and hitting is something else entirely. I feel deeply for children whose parents spank indiscriminately and violently, but tossing out the baby with the bathwater (by an across-the-board ban on spanking) is not the way to solve such a societal problem, especially one that is not widespread to begin with.

If you're going to spank, and I highly recommend that parents keep the option open, here are the ground rules.

1. The research suggests that spanking is most effective with children ages two through six, but still effective through age ten.

2. Spanking should be reserved for (a) outrageous acts of disrespect (calling parents bad names), disobedience (breaking a key rule, such as "Always let us know where you are"), or defiance (refusing to obey an instruction), or (b) stopping a rapidly escalating and/or potentially dangerous misbehavior (e.g., a tantrum, running into the street) and focusing the child's attention on a message clearly and calmly delivered from the parent.

3. Parents should spank with their hands only because then the parent's hand stings as well as the child's buttocks. This feedback will prevent a parent from going overboard with a spanking.

4. A child receiving a spanking should clearly know that parents are disappointed and strongly disapprove of what he or she has done. However, parents should never spank in the heat of anger. The child should know the parents are punishing a specific behavior, not simply flying off the handle.

5. Either before or immediately after the spanking (whichever is more appropriate), the parent should explain why the misbehavior in question is inappropriate and why the child is receiving, or has received, a spanking.

6. Two to five swats to the child's rear end are sufficient. The child should not be required to bare his or her buttocks, but outergarments can be removed, pulled down, or lifted up.

7. Only the child's buttocks should be spanked—not calves, thighs, or back.

8. After the spanking, the parent should hold, reassure, and speak lovingly to the child until he or she calms down.

9. In most cases, a spanking alone is not a sufficient disciplinary response. Remember, the behavior in question is outrageous! Parents should follow up on a spanking with a longer-lasting consequence, such as confining the child to his or her room for the remainder of the day.

It should go without saying that when a spanking is over, the air in the family has cleared and should return to normal. Parents should not act angry toward a child *after* a spanking. This does nothing but set the stage for another confrontation.

8

Making Excuses

My people are destroyed for lack of knowledge;
because you have rejected knowledge,
I will also reject you from being my priest.
Since you have forgotten the law of your God,
I also will forget your children.

—Hosea 4:6 NJB

SYNDICATED COLUMNIST William Raspberry says that the attempt to explain a person's antisocial behavior gives the person permission to continue behaving in antisocial ways. Said another way, to suggest that violence directed toward other people or property is a logical response to poverty, racism, lack of opportunity, childhood trauma, social rejection, or having been raised in a dysfunctional family gives the perpetrator an excuse to continue acting in violent ways.

The primary proponents of this modernist trend have been social activists and mental-health professionals. Take, for example, the Columbine High School killers. Immediately after the April 1999 massacre, Dylan Harris and Eric Klebold were characterized by the liberal media as "angry" at having been socially isolated by their peers. In other words, they were suffering from low self-esteem. Their anger supposedly festered and swelled inside them until it erupted in a murderous rage. Thus, if adults had been more sensitive to the troubles Harris and Klebold were experiencing and had intervened appropriately, the tragedy could have been avoided.

Contrast that pseudopsychoanalytic explanation with the one offered by a local prosecutor: Harris and Klebold didn't kill because they were angry; rather, they made themselves angry so they could kill. "They needed to work themselves up to it, to work up their sense of grudge and grievance," the prosecutor said.

Syndicated columnist Joanne Jacobs hit the nail on the head. Harris and Klebold were nothing but "punks" who made "a choice for evil." Were they loners, as characterized by the mainstream media? Hardly. They were members of a clique—the so-called Trenchcoat Mafia—that included at least twelve other students. Twelve is more good friends than I had in high school, and I never attacked anyone, much less killed people. One of the Columbine killer punks played on the soccer team until his final year in school. Another was in the drama club. Both went to a prom the weekend before their rampage. The motive, Jacob says, wasn't revenge for having been socially isolated, because they weren't. Their motive was self-generated hate. Their hate-filled act, which took the lives of thirteen innocent people and seriously wounded twenty-three others, was not a response to some set of external circumstances. It was a choice, a choice for evil.

Making Excuses at Home

Unfortunately, Raspberry and Jacobs are voices in the secular wilderness. The politically correct mainstream view of child violence was expressed by columnist Anna Quindlen in the November

29, 1999, issue of *Newsweek*. Quindlen attributes the rise of juvenile violence to adolescent depression and other emotional problems that are being largely ignored. The average citizen, Quindlen suggests, prefers to believe that kids with mental-health problems are just behaving badly and need to be disciplined more effectively and incarcerated if they commit a crime. Quindlen's solution is to demarginalize the mentally ill (by enlightening the largely ignorant, narrow-minded public) and enlarge America's mental-health-care system to provide appropriate intervention for the six million children (as estimated by the Center for Mental Health Services) who are suffering from serious emotional disturbances of one sort or another. In less than twenty column inches, Quindlen manages to blame public ignorance, the health-care insurance industry, parents who are ashamed to take troubled kids to psychologists, schools that tend to view mental-health problems as disciplinary matters, and fathers (after all, a liberal feminist has to get in a shot at men) for instilling false notions of masculinity in their sons.

> And then there are the teenagers themselves, slouching toward adulthood in a world that loves conformity. Add to the horror of creeping depression or delusions that of peer derision, the sound of the C word in the hallways: Crazy, man, he's crazy, haven't you seen him, didn't you hear? Boys, especially, still suspect that talk therapy, or even heartfelt talk, is somehow sissified, weak. Sometimes even their own fathers think so, at least until they have to identify the body.

In short, kids who do bad things are not responsible for their own behavior. They do what they do because they are ill, and the

only people who are free of blame, the only people who understand the real nature of the problem, are enlightened, compas-
sionate people like Anna Quindlen.

Granted, mental illness is a real thing. Granted, as Quindlen
asserts, "psychological intervention is cheaper than incarceration."
But does the fact that a child's mental-health problems go unnoticed
justify killing someone? Does depression render one incapable
of knowing the difference between right and wrong? No to both
questions.

Gad Czudner and Stanton Samenow are two highly respected
psychologists who have devoted most of their professional lives to
the study of children who exhibit antisocial behavior. Both have
written books on the subject. Czudner's title, *Small Criminals
Among Us: How to Recognize and Change Children's Antisocial Behavior Before They Explode,* just about says it all. These kids aren't
"sick" in any legitimate sense of the term. They are budding criminals, kids who become hooked on antisocial behavior at an early
age. The young criminal, Czudner says (echoing the latest research), seldom suffers from low self-esteem. "In fact, he tends to
think very highly of himself, but his self-esteem is based on dis-
torted values. Some kids base their self-esteem on how many kids
they can beat up in a week rather than on whether they do well in
school."

Concerning psychological treatment, Czudner (an expert on
the subject) is considerably less enthusiastic than Quindlen (a dil-
ettante) about its efficacy. He "is saddened," he writes, "that so
many professionals are still providing excuses and holding on to
psychological/psychiatric methods that, in many cases, promote
criminality rather than reduce it." Czudner sees "extreme self-
centeredness" (i.e., high self-esteem), not depression, as the crux of

habitual antisocial behavior in children. Contrast Quindlen's blame-casting view of the problem with Czudner's:

> Tedious searches for answers will only provide criminal juveniles with further excuses for their criminality. It is my contention that young offenders make a choice very early in life to go their own way and do their own thing.

Like Quindlen, Czudner believes that incarceration is less cost-effective than preventive efforts. He too believes that public awareness and educational programs for parents, teachers, and even mental-health professionals are the answer. Note, however, that Czudner holds the antisocial child responsible for his or her own behavior. That, I contend, is the bottom line.

Stanton Samenow is like-minded. In *Before It's Too Late: Why Some Kids Get into Trouble and What Parents Can Do About It*, he says an assumption is often made that youngsters become delinquent because they lack adequate nurturing (referring to so-called "attachment disorders"), that they are the product of uncaring, indifferent, and irresponsible parents. How then, Samenow asks, does one explain that the majority of children from bad homes do *not* turn to crime, or that some children from warm, loving families become menaces to society? The only explanation is *choice*— the exercise of individual free will.

Like Czudner, Samenow believes parents, schools, and professionals should be trained to recognize the antisocial child at an early age and act authoritatively—in tough yet loving ways— to stop the bad behavior and instill proper moral values. "Once early manifestations of antisocial behavior are recognized, it is possible to work toward preventing these from becoming fixed patterns," he says, nodding in Quindlen's direction. But Samenow, unlike Quindlen, assigns responsibility to those truly responsible: "If we continue to look to theories as to why these children become criminals, then everyone and everything becomes the culprit *except the actual perpetrator of the crime*" (italics mine). Well-intentioned attempts by mental-health professionals to generate sociopsychological theories concerning a child's bad behavior turn the *victimizer* into a *victim,* which is exactly what Quindlen has done.

Samenow says violent children are neither confused nor out of touch with reality. "They understand the difference between right and wrong, and they understand the consequences to themselves and to others." From an early age, the violent child makes choices (that word again!) about living, craves "high voltage excitement" and the forbidden, and disdains socially acceptable behavior as boring, stupid, and wimpy.

Samenow and Czudner are right, but they are voices crying in the wilderness. Their words are being drowned out by those of thousands of mental-health "experts" who earn their livelihoods making excuses for antisocial children. These excuses are called diagnoses, of which the two most glaring contemporary examples are Attention Deficit Hyperactivity Disorder (ADHD) and Oppositional Defiant Disorder (ODD). In both cases, we are talking about children who will not do what they are told. In both cases, child psychiatrists and child psychologists have actively promoted the notion that these children are thralls to biological kinks of one sort or another. Accordingly, these children are considered incapable of controlling their outrageous behaviors—lying, cursing, defiance, aggression, destructiveness, and so on. The biological factors in question include such nebulous pseudoscientific concepts as "chemical imbalance," "genetic predisposition," and "minimal brain dysfunction." Mental-health practitioners have hood-winked the general public (and in many cases themselves) into believing that these ideas are founded on scientific facts. It may surprise the reader to learn there is absolutely no convincing evidence that such things as genetic predispositions exist, or even if they did, that they would render a child incapable of controlling his or her behavior.

Nonetheless, psychologists and psychiatrists write book after book and article after article claiming that children who behave in dangerous, self-defeating, antisocial ways "can't help it." The children in question are supposedly driven by malevolent genes, bio-chemical excesses or inadequacies, and invisible brain lesions to commit acts of violence, deceit, larceny, and so on.

One such book is *The Explosive Child* by psychologist Ross Greene. The sort of child in question is what Grandma would have termed an "undisciplined brat"—a child who frequently throws temper tantrums, is often belligerently defiant, and is prone to becoming verbally and physically aggressive when frustrated. Grandma would have made no excuses for this child. She would have prescribed powerful, consistent discipline. Greene, however, maintains that such children can't help behaving the way they behave; they no more choose to behave in antisocial ways than another child would choose to have a reading disability (as if a perceptual problem and a behavior problem can be equated). He says they have a brain-chemistry problem that makes them incapable of exercising appropriate self-restraint. For that reason, their parents have to put all preconceived notions of discipline on the shelf. Hard-nosed discipline—taking privileges away, verbal reprimands, grounding, spanking—is likely to make matters worse. Greene says that the explosive child's parents must be "flexible." They must try to avoid situations and circumstances that will trigger their child's explosive nature by steering him or her around those situations (make compensations). They must reduce the demands they place on the child (enable). They must negotiate and compromise with the child (compensate and enable some more). For example, instead of saying "no" to the child's request to spend a school night at a friend's house, they should talk the problem through and reach a compromise.

"This is not giving in," Greene says. "This is parents proposing a problem and helping a child collaborate on a solution. Look at it this way: What's more important, blind adherence to authority or resolving conflict?"

Greene is proposing that the parents of the explosive child put him or her at the center of attention and tiptoe around as if the child is a time bomb that will explode at the slightest jostle. If this isn't giving in to the child in order to avoid a showdown, I don't know what is. And Greene's dichotomy of "blind adherence to authority or resolving conflict" is disingenuous at best. Obedience to legitimate parental authority is not "blind adherence." Teaching a child to obey is by no means incompatible with teaching a child to think independently and use pro-social means of resolving conflict. But just as children must learn to walk before they can run, children must learn to obey authority figures before they can be taught to negotiate with them. Greene is actually up to the old demonization of traditional parenting that psychologists have been engaged in for more than a generation. The fact is, it was rare fifty years ago to encounter one of Greene's explosive kids. Traditional parenting had exorcised self-centeredness by the time the child was three or four (at the latest!) and replaced it with self-control. Today's ubiquitous explosive child is a product of the very sort of parenting Greene recommends: weak, cooperative, relationship-oriented. Like many of his colleagues in the mental-health profession, Greene has blinders on. His solution for the explosive child amounts to the problem. Weak parenting produced this epidemic and Greene says more of the same will eliminate it. That makes no sense at all.

As for his "brain chemistry" hypothesis, it's bunk, pure and simple. The only way to determine if such a thing is true is surgery to invade the child's brain, take tissue samples, and analyze them. Needless to say, Greene is speculating. Furthermore, his speculation is hardly scientific. There is no good evidence that an "imbalance" of chemicals in the brain can render an otherwise intelligent child incapable of following instructions or coping with the word *no*. And let's keep in mind that these so-called explosive kids can always be sweet and loving if they want something from someone. What Greene talks about is actually a manipulative, self-absorbed psychopath in the making (if not already made)—one of Czudner's "small criminals."

Greene's book is a prime example of how today's mental-health practitioners turn victimizers into victims and use pseudoscientific theories to provide excuses for bad behavior, of professionals who are enablers instead of educators.

But why, if there is no good evidence that otherwise normal, healthy children can suffer from biological defects that render responsible decision-making impossible, do mental-health professionals persist in promulgating such hogwash? Because it keeps them in business.

First, if parents believe that by taking a misbehaving child to a therapist, blame for the child's behavior is going to be cast on them, they aren't likely to seek professional help. Second, if they make an appointment and hear the therapist say their parenting is at fault, they aren't likely to return for a second appointment. Third, by telling parents that the problem is biological, the therapist can stretch the treatment out indefinitely. If the problem is biological, it can't be cured, it can only be treated. The treatment, furthermore, will need to be ongoing—perhaps for the rest of the child's life—and involve medical interventions, which add further cost to the "treatment plan."

The problem is that most mental-health professionals don't really believe in *choice*, in old-fashioned free will. They don't believe in it *because* it's old-fashioned. More specifically, it's scriptural. It's straight out of the Book of Genesis, and psychology prides itself on having risen above such "primitive myths." Where antisocial behavior is concerned, and especially when the perpetrator is a child, mental-health professionals have been trained to believe in deterministic explanations, of which there are two.

> 1. The child's behavior is a logical, albeit unconscious, response to problems in his or her family—an alcoholic parent, divorce, abuse, and so on through the list of family dysfunctions. The child in this case is "crying for help," not just for him- or herself but for parents and siblings as well.
>
> 2. The behavior results from biological factors, in which case the child is the victim of malevolent chemicals produced in the body that drive him or her to act badly.

Note that in neither case can the child help behaving in antisocial ways. In the first instance, he or she is little more than a leaf blown about by the ongoing winds of family history. In the second, the child is a leaf in a biological windstorm. Interestingly, mental-health professionals generally avoid discussion of why the child in question always manages to behave properly if some reward is involved, a new bicycle perhaps. The question implies something most psychologists—Samenow and Czudner being notable exceptions—don't want to consider: *choice*.

If the antisocial child is *choosing* to behave badly, if, as Samenow says, the child *knows* the difference between right and wrong and *knows* how bad behavior affects other people, this is not a psychological problem, is it? It is a *moral* issue. It follows that if the problem is moral rather than psychological (as Samenow and Czudner seem to believe), it doesn't fall within the domain of the mental-health professional. Take it from a psychologist: That is extremely threatening to most of my colleagues. As Czudner asserts, many mental-health professionals are in the business of making excuses and providing "treatments" that promote, rather than reduce, antisocial behavior in children. It is not in the best interests of violent, antisocial children that mental-health professionals make such excuses. As such, the mental-health professions themselves must be held significantly responsible for the rising tide of violent behavior in children.

Making Excuses in School

Consider the following sequence of events: First, mental-health professionals identify a new behavior "disorder," claiming it is nearly epidemic. Then they use the media to promote the myth that the disorder is largely, if not entirely, a matter of biology. The biological theory supports the nefarious notion that children supposedly "afflicted" with the new disorder cannot help doing what they do—disobeying, lying, stealing, hitting, cursing, screaming at adults, and so on. Next, parent support groups spring up all over the country, followed shortly thereafter by the formation of a national organization to coordinate state-level activities and bring the disorder to the attention of the larger public. The national organization hires lobbyists to educate state and national legislators concerning the nature of the disorder and encourage them to designate the children so afflicted as eligible for special education services as well as special considerations under the Individuals with Disabilities Education Act (IDEA) of 1994. The lobbying is successful and, the next thing you know, little psychopaths are not only proliferating in America's public schools but are protected from effective discipline by federal law.

It's fairly common knowledge that today's public school teachers and administrators are often afraid to discipline misbehaving students. After all, discipline might bring on a lawsuit. Ironically, the more a child misbehaves and the more outrageous the misbehavior, the more reason teachers and administrators have for not disciplining. This has created a "damned if they do, damned if they don't" set of circumstances for public school educators, as exemplified in the following true story.

In the spring of 1999, a divided Supreme Court ruled 5–4 that a Georgia school responded "inadequately" to a fifth-grade girl's complaints of being sexually harassed by a male classmate. There's no doubt the boy sexually harassed her and there's no doubt the girl suffered emotionally and her grades dropped. But did the school violate federal law?

The 1972 law in question states that no person "shall, on the basis of sex, be excluded from participation in, be denied the benefits of, or be subjected to discrimination under" any education program receiving federal funds. Justices O'Connor, Souter, Stevens,

Ginsberg, and Breyer demonstrated an inability to think clearly about "feminist" issues by ruling that the 1972 language applies when a school shows deliberate indifference to "severe, pervasive, and offensive" harassment of which the school has "actual knowledge." No matter that the law says nothing about sexual harassment in grade school. O'Connor maintained that it was implied and, even more incredibly, that Congress meant to imply it. (One might ask, If Congress meant to imply it, why then wasn't it simply stated?)

Justices Kennedy, Scalia, Rehnquist, and Thomas dissented, saying that since Congress was not explicit about including grade school sexual harassment, the states had no way of knowing what sort of response was adequate. Kennedy also noted that the ruling places schools in a double bind. The Individuals with Disabilities Education Act, he pointed out, "places strict limits on the ability of schools to take disciplinary actions against students with behavior disorders, *even if the disability was not diagnosed prior to the incident triggering discipline*" (emphasis mine). In other words, if a school disciplines a child who is *later* diagnosed with a nouveau behavioral "disability," the child's parents can sue.

In case you think I'm kidding, here's a sample of IDEA's disciplinary guidelines and requirements, as published by the Albuquerque Public Schools (September 1999):

Schools can remove (suspend or expel) a special education student for up to ten consecutive school days at any time for any violation of school rules, as long as there is not a pattern of suspension (multiple suspensions for the same behavior without attempting interventions, or multiple suspensions in a relatively short time period). Neither the statute nor final regulations impose absolute limits on the number of days a student can be removed from his or her current placement in a school year.

This guideline clearly states that a misbehaving student who is a recipient of special education services can be disciplined with suspension or expulsion. But two paragraphs later, the document reads:

A student cannot be long term suspended or expelled for behavior that is a manifestation of his/her disability.

And there you have it—the double bind. A school can discipline a special education student if, and only if, the problem behavior is not related to the student's "disability." For example, if a boy who's been diagnosed with Attention Deficit Disorder (ADD) gets mad at a teacher for reprimanding him and punches the teacher in the face, the student cannot be disciplined in any meaningful way because problems with self-control are part and parcel of "having" ADD. He didn't *mean* to hit the teacher, he just couldn't help himself. Instead of being disciplined, instead of paying a price for what he did, the student is referred for more counseling sessions, and the level of his medication is adjusted. This makes it ever more likely that the student will hit a teacher again or perhaps do something even more outrageous. And there's even more:

These disciplinary requirements also apply to students "suspected" of having a disability. "Suspicion of the existence of a disability" is triggered by (a) a parent requesting an evaluation, (b) a parent expressing a written concern of need for special education, (c) evidence in school, behaviorally or in performance, of a student's need for special education, or (d) school personnel having expressed concern about a student's behavior or performance.

In effect, these IDEA guidelines make it risky for a public school to discipline *any* student for *any* misbehavior.

In the Georgia case, it is reasonable to assume that a fifth-grade boy who sexually harasses a classmate in a "severe, persistent, and objectively offensive" manner is a budding psychopath. How is the school supposed to discipline this boy so that his harassment stops, thus preventing litigation from the girl's parents, but also in a manner which prevents litigation from *the boy's* parents? Let's face it. Some parents will only accept that their child is emotionally disturbed if the diagnosis comes with the promise of winning megabucks in the litigation lottery.

Justice Kennedy warned, and rightly so, that this landmark decision threatens to turn "every disciplinary decision into a jury question."

National Organization for Women (NOW) president Patricia Ireland, commenting on the case, said, "Nobody, even feminists, wants to make a federal case out of a food fight in the cafeteria. The behavior we're talking about goes way beyond snapping girls' bra straps."

I doubt it, but we'll see.

9

Is Dad the Culprit?

Grandchildren are the crown of old men,
and the glory of sons is their fathers'.

—Proverbs 17:6 NJB

IN SEPTEMBER OF 1999, the following Associated Press article was picked up by countless newspapers across the country.

EXPERTS: BOYS FASHIONED FOR VIOLENCE

Raising boys to be strong and silent is promoting the outbreak of mass school shootings and a broader, smoldering climate of despair among male teenagers, experts suggest.

"I think we have a national crisis of boys in America," said William Pollack, a psychologist at Harvard Medical School.

He and several other researchers on Friday discussed violent boys at the annual meeting of the American Psychological Association. They were responding partly to public concern over recent mass killings at schools.

In April, two students killed 12 classmates and a teacher before committing suicide at Columbine High School in Littleton, Colo. Other school shootings have struck Georgia, Mississippi, Kentucky, Arkansas and Oregon. The increase in

---

such crimes is statistically small. There were two school homicides with multiple victims in 1992 but six last year—and they were largely at suburban schools. The number of victims increased from four to 16. The psychologists said American boys are still reared largely in keeping with the traditional code of male toughness, which encourages boys to take action but squelches expressions of feeling and gestures of physical affection by and toward boys.

"You can punch one another, but you can't really have an affectionate touch," said Dan Kindlon, a psychologist at Harvard School of Public Health.

The researchers said cross-cultural studies demonstrate a clear link between violent societies and those that treat children with little physical warmth, according to University of Miami researcher Tiffany Field.

"For some boys who are not allowed tears, they will cry with their fists or they will cry with bullets," added Pollack.

The psychologists said such rearing makes it hard for boys to handle adversity and lays the foundation for a spectrum of depression and violence among teenagers ranging from male bullying to murder.

The psychologists pressed for big changes in how parents and educators treat boys. They said parents should give physical affection freely to boys, allow them to show their feelings and reject the widespread belief that boys are inherently more violent than girls.

The psychologists urged educators to foster friendlier schools, provide more counseling and—despite worries about false accusations of sex abuse—not shirk from physically comforting a hurt child.

This is the same "traditional parenting is bad for children" drum psychologists have been beating for thirty years. Psychologist Thomas Gordon, author of several self-esteem-based parenting tomes, including the parenting bible of the 1970s, *Parent Effectiveness Training*, actually went so far as to attribute nearly every social evil to the psychic abuse inherent in traditional character-based parenting. The idea was bogus in 1971, when Gordon published his first best-selling book, and it's still bogus. First, absolutely no evidence exists to support the notion that traditional parenting turns good kids into bad kids. If anything, traditional parenting turns potentially bad—*really, really* bad—kids into good kids. Second, all the available evidence suggests that traditional parenting did a better job of curbing aggression in children than does nouveau psychological (self-esteem-based) parenting. Rates of child violence have increased sharply over the last three decades, ever since self-esteem-based parenting took hold in the United States. Third, if the problem is with the manner in which males are being raised, then how do we explain the fact that *female* violence has been increasing dramatically over the past few decades? Girls are now doing things that only boys did thirty years ago. One respected researcher, a professor of criminal justice at Indiana University, estimates that in ten to twenty years, rates of male and female violence will be approximately equal. Some interesting tragic facts about the rise of violent crime among female juveniles:

- Teenage girls committed a quarter of all juvenile crime in 1995, and more than 700,000 were arrested, pushing the rate of crimes committed by girls up faster than that of boys.

- The trend in female juvenile delinquency is toward crimes that are increasingly violent. Girls are now more likely to be arrested for armed robbery, assault, and gang activity than for prostitution, forgery, and simple theft.
- In one year, 1994–95, girls' arrests increased 3 percent for aggravated assault (vs. a 4.5 percent decrease for boys) and 7.7 percent for other assaults (vs. an increase of 1.8 percent for boys).

It is very dramatic to say that boys who are not allowed to cry will "cry with their fists or cry with bullets," but it doesn't compute. Since the mid-1960s when American parents began embracing a child-rearing philosophy that emphasized allowing children to freely express feelings, rates of childhood and teen depression have risen sharply—by some estimates, as much as tenfold. Furthermore, the premise of the argument—that many boys are not allowed to display feelings—is not only unsubstantiated but also completely untrue. In 1993, psychologist Diana Baumrind found the vast majority of parents expressed lots of love to their children. If one assumes what is commonsensical, that parents who express lots of love also tend to encourage expression of feelings in their children, only one conclusion is possible: most boys are permitted, even encouraged, to express their feelings. The further implication, echoing Anna Quindlen (see chapter 8), that the typical father fosters violent behavior by not allowing boys to be sensitive, is a lie. The psychologists in question are surely aware that *all* the research confirms that a boy is far less likely to engage in any anti-social behavior if he lives with his father.

The psychologists mentioned in the Associated Press article are cutting their theory out of whole cloth. But why would a panel of respected psychologists make up a theory of this sort out of thin air? In the first place, public opinion of psychology is on the wane. People are sick of psychobabble, which includes most psychological discourse. So the profession needs some good press and in the present example managed to get it. In the second place, one must understand that making things up has been the norm in psychology since its inception. Sigmund Freud's theories were all made up. He had no scientific evidence to support them. For the most part, psychological theories are impossible to prove or disprove. If a theory sounds good and is sensationalistic, the media pay attention to it, and it's only a matter of time before the public accepts it as fact.

The theory that boys become violent because they aren't allowed to express their feelings is put forth at a time when the nation is still reeling from the mass murder at Columbine High School. Never mind that it is nothing more than a theory, and a bad one at that. It serves a purpose, but it does not serve the truth. The mental-health profession has promoted a subtle antifamily (or, more accurately, anti-*traditional family*) agenda for most of the past twenty years. According to the party line, the traditional family is an inherently pathological unit because it represents the interests of the so-called patriarchy—male domination of society. The father supposedly rules by bullying his wife and kids and (often) sexually abusing his daughters, which is why everyone who grew up in a traditional family needs therapy, which the makers of this mythology will be happy to provide for upwards of $100 per 45-minute hour.

The truth about fathers is that the presence of a biological father in the home greatly increases his children's chances of success by any measurement—academic, social, emotional, behavioral. Children who grow up without their fathers are at significant risk for all sorts of problems, including academic failure, conduct disorders, depression, suicide, and delinquency. According to David Blankenhorn, author of *Fatherless America,* the typical father does not teach his boys to be tough and insensitive or to hold in their emotions. Quite the contrary—he models respect for women, sensitivity to other people's feelings, and appropriate ways of expressing feelings. The idea that fathers are too hard on their sons, thus turning them into emotional dwarfs who cry with their fists or with bullets, is a canard. A live-in father, far from being dangerous to a child's upbringing, is an insurance policy no child can afford to be without.

This last point was emphasized by a decade-long study funded by the National Institute of Mental Health. This research, conducted between 1989 and 1999, revealed that divorce more than doubles the risk for adjustment problems in children. But the most alarming news was that the risk of serious depression following divorce was significantly higher for boys than for girls, even *when the post-divorce situation was fairly ideal* (i.e., the mother and father got along, the mother's remarriage was good, the children got along with their stepfather, and so on.) The authors speculated that "perhaps even optimal post-divorce circumstances are not sufficient to compensate for the sadness experienced by boys because of the departure of their father from the home." When dads continue to be highly involved with their sons following divorce, the risk of behavior problems in boys is reduced considerably.

In short, dads are good for children. They're especially good for their sons. Propaganda to the contrary on the part of establishment psychologists or liberal pundits is nothing more than babble.

Another example of how the media miss the point concerning America's child crisis was reflected in *Newsweek*'s May 11, 1998, cover story, "How to Build a Better Boy."

The article began by correctly pointing out that boys are far more likely than girls to:

- be diagnosed with various conduct disorders, attention deficit disorder, and learning disabilities
- drop out of school
- abuse drugs and alcohol
- engage in high-risk behaviors
- do violence to others and to themselves

But girls are far more likely than boys to become seriously depressed, develop life-threatening anorexia nervosa, and engage in sexual intercourse before age twelve. Ignoring the big picture, that *all* our children, not just boys, are having more problems than Grandma thought possible, *Newsweek* proposed that America is having a "boy crisis." The explanation for this contrivance amounted to (a) boys will be boys (they've always been more rowdy and relatively difficult), (b) fathers aren't sufficiently involved with their sons, and (c) parents inadvertently deprive boys of sufficient affection and attention. To solve America's boy problem, *Newsweek* said (a) parents need to accept that boys are more active and aggressive, aren't as verbal, and don't do as well in school until the higher grades, (b) parents, especially fathers, need to be more involved with and affectionate toward their sons, and (c) everyone who has children or works with them needs to recognize the "crisis points" that mark a male child's development and respond with appropriate support and guidance.

Newsweek must have spoken to some members of the American Psychological Association or they would have gotten their facts straight concerning fathers. America's boys, who weren't in crisis forty years ago, are in trouble today largely because adults don't discipline children as well as they once did. That also applies to America's girls. In fact, the general weakening of child discipline was reflected in the article. After ignoring the discipline issue for five pages, *Newsweek* advised parents not to punish in anger and to try and resolve "disputes" by talking them through with their children.

The fact is, today's boys are considerably more undisciplined than their fathers were because American parents have been led to believe that any discipline problem can be resolved by talking. By the time a boy or girl has developed a full-blown behavior problem, the situation is already past the point where talking is going to help. Parents need to *act*—quickly, decisively, and emphatically.

The article ends on the following flat note: "Boys will be boys. And we have to let them." Actually, even "boyish" behavior requires limits. Boys can still be boys if they aren't allowed to jump their bikes over deep concrete culverts, stage kick-boxing matches in the back yard, jump on furniture, or stomp their feet and yell when told to do something. When it comes to "boyish" misbehavior, parents must keep in mind that the operative word is *misbehavior;* being a boy is no excuse for being disruptive, disobedient, aggressive, or hotheaded. Last but not least, parents must realize that boyishly powerful misbehavior requires equally powerful discipline—not harsh, but *convincing.* The problem with too many of today's girls and boys is they've never been convinced that adults know where to stand or when and how to deliver.

10

The-Media-Turn-'Em-into-Killers Theory

For they eat the bread of wickedness
and drink the wine of violence.

—Proverbs 4:17 AV

THE April 1999 killings in Littleton, Colorado, incited a finger-pointing frenzy, and one of the targets was the mass media that supposedly "glorify" violence. Actually, "are obsessed with" is more like it.

Here are the raw statistics: By age five, the average American couch potato trainee is watching close to three hours of television per day, more than one thousand hours per year. He or she goes to first grade having watched more than four thousand hours of television! By age twelve, that same child is watching nearly five hours of television a day and has seen an astonishing 8,000 killings. In the average American home, television is on more than seven hours per day. Fifty-four percent of American children have televisions in their rooms. American children watch two hours of television for every hour spent in school. In one survey of children ages four to six, more than half stated they preferred watching TV to spending time with their parents. Prime-time television programming averages some five violent acts per hour, whereas children's Saturday morning programs average from twenty to twenty-five violent acts per hour.

Does watching televised violence predispose to violent behavior? On this question, nearly all studies done to date *have* found a relationship.

- In response to questions like, "Suppose you are riding your bicycle down the street and some other child comes up and pushes you off your bicycle; what would you do?" children who were heavy watchers of television violence were more likely than light watchers to select aggressive responses.
- A study done in the early 1970s found that children who had watched violent programming demonstrated a heightened willingness to hurt other children.
- Children judged to be already somewhat aggressive became even more so after watching Batman and Superman cartoons.
- Children who seem to enjoy watching violence on television are more likely to be aggressive than children who become distressed when viewing television violence.
- One study suggests that early preference for violent television programming and other media is a significant predictor of aggressive and generally antisocial behavior in late adolescence and young adulthood.
- Young girls who in the 1970s often watched shows featuring aggressive heroines *(Charlie's Angels, The Bionic Woman)* have grown up to be more aggressive adults—involved in more shoving matches, choking incidents, and knife fights—than women who had watched few or none of these sorts of shows as children.

Based on evidence of this sort, the National Institute of Mental Health issued a policy statement in 1982 which said, in part, that

> violence on television does lead to aggressive behavior in children and teenagers who watch the programs. This conclusion is based on laboratory experiments and on field studies. Not all children become aggressive, of course, but the correlations between violence and aggression are positive. In magnitude, television violence is as strongly correlated with aggressive behavior as any other behavioral variable that has been measured. The research question has moved from asking whether or not there is an effect to seeking explanations for the effect.

More recently, researcher Leonard Eron of the University of Michigan summarized his findings before a 1992 congressional committee on television violence:

> There can no longer be any doubt that heavy exposure to televised violence is one of the causes of aggressive behavior, crime, and violence in society. The evidence comes from both the laboratory and real-life studies. Television violence affects youngsters of all ages, of both genders, at all socioeconomic levels and all levels of intelligence. The effect is not limited to children who are already disposed to being aggressive and is not restricted to this country. The causal effect of television violence on aggression, even though it is not very large, exists. It cannot be denied or explained away. We have demonstrated this causal effect outside the laboratory in real life among many different

children. We have come to believe that a vicious cycle exists in which television violence makes children more aggressive and these aggressive children turn to watching more violence to justify their own behavior.

Two of the most outspoken critics of media violence are former West Point professor and Army Ranger Lt. Col. David Grossman (USA, Ret.), and parent counselor Gloria DeGaetano, authors of *Stop Teaching Our Kids to Kill: A Call to Action Against TV, Movie and Video Game Violence.* Grossman and DeGaetano say we are "raising generations of children who learn at a very early age to associate horrific violence with pleasure and excitement—a dangerous association for a civilized society." They decry not only the fact that video-game violence is becoming increasingly realistic but also that children become active participants (as opposed to simply passive watchers) in video games and learn, through that insidious electronic process, to enjoy killing and mutilating, if only at a fantasy level.

In previous books like *A Family of Value,* I have maintained that video games are addictive in that a child who obtains a certain score is compelled to better it and is likely to become obsessed with doing so. Grossman and DeGaetano agree, adding that violence is an integral aspect of the addiction, pointing out that a child's score is often a body count.

Children with video games, which are usually hooked up to televisions in their rooms (where parental supervision is virtually nil), play an average of ninety minutes per day, or more than ten hours per week, thirty hours per month, or nearly four hundred hours per year. That's more time spent playing at violence than being engaged in any other single extracurricular activity! And it's not just the violence that counts. It's also the disturbing fact that these kids are not doing other more constructive things with their time. They are not learning how to negotiate conflicts with their peers in peaceable ways. They are not learning appropriate social skills. Instead, they're losing themselves in games that reinforce delusions of power and dominance of the-ends-justify-the-means sort. More often than not, unfortunately, their parents welcome the amount of time they spend in video-game play, for reasons ranging from "it keeps her out of our hair" to "at least we know where he is and what he's doing."

Certain video games, Grossman and DeGaetano assert, are actually killing simulators that teach children killing skills in the same way the Apollo astronauts learned to fly in space without leaving the ground. The army uses Multipurpose Arcade Combat Simulators (MACS), which are nothing more than modified Super Nintendo games. The Fire Arms Training Simulator (FATS) used by many law enforcement agencies in this country to train officers in weaponry skills is more or less identical to the ultraviolent video game "Time Crisis." Military and law enforcement agencies are not at all happy that these highly realistic games (some even let the child experience recoil when firing the "gun") are available to children.

At least three of the 1990s school killers were highly involved with violent video games. According to reports, Dylan Klebold and Eric Harris, the Columbine High School murderers, were obsessed with such violent video games as the highly popular "Doom," as was Michael Carneal, the Paducah, Kentucky, shooter.

Grossman quotes Dr. Donald Shifrin, a pediatrician, as saying, "There is no need to have a video-game system in the house, especially for young children. There is no middle ground for me on this. I view it as a black-and-white issue like bike helmets for safety."

I agree. I would also add that no child should have a bedroom television or a computer hooked up to the Internet. In my estimation, it is unconscionable for a parent to turn a child's room into an entertainment center. In the first place, this encourages the child to become isolated. In the second, it reduces parental supervision of the content the child is accessing to a minimum. Grossman and DeGaetano suggest no more than ten hours of total screen time (computers, television, video games, videos) per week. I say that's still too much. I'd draw the line at five. And, as Willie and I did when our kids lived at home, I'd recommend that every parent carefully monitor and control all content, cutting out movies and television programs with gratuitously violent content. If parents enjoy video games, and there's a unit in the home as a consequence, I strongly urge that children of any age never be allowed to play. Instead, I recommend slow-paced computer games that require problem-solving skills. But again, I would not under any circumstances allow even these sorts of games to dominate a child's discretionary time—time during which children should be developing social skills and learning to solve real-life problems.

Some researchers maintain that violent movies, television programs, and video games only contribute to violent tendencies in certain already undersocialized children. They believe that violence is essentially in the eye of the beholder—some kids can watch or play at it with no effect while for other kids, those already possessing previolent or violent personalities, violent media is toxic. I agree with that assessment as well. To me, however, the critical question is not, "Is my child one of the kids for whom violence on the media is or will become toxic?" but, rather, "Is it healthy for my child to view graphic depictions of violence in movies and on television or play video games in which killing is presented as sport?" I don't think any thinking person would say such things are healthy for kids. Childhood simply should not be saturated with violent images. At the very least, such images desensitize a child to the horror of violence, and in an increasingly violent society that is definitely something we cannot afford.

I have one significant point of disagreement with Grossman and DeGaetano. They believe the problem of media violence requires more government intervention in the form of laws, regulation, and restriction. Along those lines, a recent *USA Today*/CNN/Gallup Poll found that Americans overwhelmingly believe the federal government should do more to regulate violence in the media. Thomas Jefferson must be rolling over in his grave. Few citizens want to accept that problems of the sort under discussion are not going to be solved by politicians. Prohibition has never worked. The problem of media violence can only be truly solved at the grass-roots level, by the sort of people who read this book: you.

You believe children are exposed to too much violence on television? Do something about it! Do whatever is necessary to make sure your children never again see a violent act on your television. Get rid of the TV sets in their rooms—give 'em away to a homeless shelter. Cancel the cable and watch only videotapes and/or videodiscs. If you just can't feel like a normal human being without cable, purchase a lock-out device (or use the lock-out feature on your set) and cancel every channel except those that guarantee nonviolent programming.

You don't approve of the violence in video games? What are you waiting for? Don't let your kids play any video games but those you've screened. Be the Video Game Censor from Hades! Better yet, don't let 'em play any video games at all. Help them discover what a normal childhood is all about.

You think a lot of today's pop musicians promote violence, promiscuous sex, and sexism? So do I. Make it a rule that you have to listen to and approve of any and all music they bring into your home before they can listen to it. If lyrics are included, read 'em carefully. When you find something that is even the slightest bit offensive to you, put it in the garbage.

You're concerned about violent and pornographic material on the Internet? Go to an electronics store and purchase a gadget that prevents your child from turning on your home computer. Don't just sit there and wring your hands—do something!

There are those who would love nothing more than to see the federal government empowered to appropriate certain parental responsibilities. The bad news is that apparently a good number of parents would rather Big Daddy Washington took on any responsibilities that entail more than slight inconvenience. The good news is that this won't happen as long as enough parents are willing to shoulder their responsibilities—all of them.

Part Two

The Solutions:
Where Do We Go from Here?

11

Teach Manners
and Morals

*"In everything, therefore, treat people the
same way you want them to treat you,
for this is the Law and the Prophets."*

—Matthew 7:12 NJB

In *Toward a Meaningful Life: The Wisdom of the Rebbe* (adapted by
Simon Jacobson), the late Rabbi Menachem Mendel Schneerson,
leader of the Lubavitcher movement of Chassidic Judaism for most
of the last half of the twentieth century, states unequivocally that a
child's character education should take priority over his academic
education. In fact, the esteemed rebbe says all other educational
efforts are basically meaningless unless built on the solid foundation of good character.

In the movie *Blast from the Past,* one of the characters discovers, as he puts it, "Good manners are a way of showing respect
for others" and not, as he'd previously thought, a means of calling
attention to oneself. He also discovers that it is most important to
do all you can to help the people around you feel comfortable.

Character and manners are inseparable. Good manners are
symptomatic of good character, and the linchpin of good character

111

is respect for others, as reflected by good manners. That one scene in *Blast from the Past* caused me to wonder if perhaps the screen-writer had read the rebbe's wisdom teachings.

Today's parents would certainly say they want their children to possess good character, but how many actually take the time to teach proper manners? Setting a good example is not enough. Teaching manners requires instruction, and instruction—reminding, explaining, correcting, or rehearsing—takes time. The world would definitely be a better place if parents took even half the time they spent driving their children to various extracurricular pursuits and taught manners instead.

Teaching manners to preschool children—the earlier the better—pays off in numerous ways. I have nothing but personal experience to support what I'm about to say, but I'll bet my stock portfolio that the well-mannered child is going to be more obedient, do better in school, and get along far better with siblings and friends. Not to mention that the child's parents will receive lots of positive feedback from other parents, teachers, neighbors, and even strangers. Not to mention that, for all those reasons, the child in question will be much happier than he or she otherwise would have been.

The first manners a child should learn, by the age of four, are (in no particular order):

- Saying "please," "thank you," and "you're welcome" when appropriate
- Saying "I'm sorry" after hurting someone, either physically or emotionally
- Saying "excuse me" when appropriate (but see below for when it's *not* appropriate)

• Sharing toys and other possessions freely
• Saying "Yes, ma'am/sir" and "No, ma'am/sir" when appropriate
• Not interrupting adult conversations, even with "excuse me"

I assign a lot of weight to that last one for several reasons. First, in learning not to interrupt, a child learns patience. Second, learning not to interrupt strengthens respect for adults. Third, I am highly annoyed when a child interrupts an adult conversation.

It would appear that many, if not most, of today's parents teach their children it's perfectly all right to interrupt two adults in conversation, for any reason at all, by simply walking up and saying, "Excuse me!" I gather this because when a child simply walks up and begins talking, it's usually the case that the child's parent will stop talking to me, look down at the child, and say, "What have I taught you to say?" At which point the child says, "Excuse me."

I said as much at a recent talk in Rancho Santa Fe, California. Afterward, a well-spoken gentleman from South Africa introduced himself and remarked that he too was both annoyed and cynically amused by parents who tolerated their children's interruptions. He told me that, in South Africa, one of the first things a child is taught is how to be recognized when he or she wants to speak. Suppose the child walks into the general area where the adults are talking and stands a respectful distance—say, eight feet—away. Any fool, he said, can tell the child wants to say something. When the adults reach a point where a pause in their conversation feels natural, one (the child's parent, usually) will turn to the child and say, "Yes?" at which point the child will speak.

Oh, how civilized! But wait—that is exactly what I was taught as a child. And, I daresay, so were most of my peers. How is it that children who were taught this important social formality, one that speaks so loudly to the quality of their overall upbringing, fail to teach it to their own kids?

Many of today's parents think parenting is taking a child to play in a soccer game and watching from the stands. That's not parenting. Parenting is not a spectator sport, it's hands on—a verb, in today's vernacular.

Today's parents are likely to expend a lot of energy doing things that have little if any long-term value to a child and only a little energy doing things that are of lasting value and would make their job easier in the long run. Like taking time to teach a child—by explaining and rehearsing, for example—how to be recognized when two adults are engaged in conversation.

I would suggest that the fellow from South Africa had the right idea. Teach your child to stand a respectful distance from adults who are talking and wait, silently and in a state of stillness, until acknowledged. And, when it comes right down to it, gradually increase the wait until the child has learned to be silent and still for upwards of five minutes.

"So what's the child to do if there's a genuine emergency?"

How about giving your child a hand signal to use in such circumstances? And, let's face it, what a child considers an emergency is not always an emergency or even close to it.

"And what should I do when my child interrupts, even after learning the art of waiting?"

I really don't think there's a formula for that one, other than to make sure your child learns that misbehavior has consequences: an early bedtime that evening, a canceled sleepover that was to take place later in the week. Whatever you do, do something your child will remember.

And don't forget to say how proud you are when he or she does the right thing. Punishment is a necessary aspect of discipline, but without equal amounts of praise it does nothing but breed contempt.

I cannot leave a discussion of manners without emphasizing the importance of teaching children religious values, otherwise known as morals. Parents, take your children to church or synagogue or mosque. And if you get them involved in just *one* after-school activity, make it a religious youth group run by a competent young adult or a married couple who are themselves a model of marital devotion. All studies clearly indicate that children who attend a church, regardless of denomination, children who acquire a solid grounding in moral values through ongoing moral instruction, are far less likely to engage in antisocial behavior of any kind, especially through their critical teen years. They are less likely to use drugs, engage in premarital sex, be arrested for any reason, develop behavior problems, or experience academic problems and far more likely, as adults, to enter into marriages that succeed. This has been confirmed over and over again in research, for example, by the National Institute of Healthcare Research, the Heritage Foundation, and the national Longitudinal Study on Adolescent Health (LSAH); by researchers at the University of Nebraska and Arizona State University West; and in research done through the National Center on Addiction and Substance Abuse (CASA) at Columbia University. Here's what LSAH researcher Michael Resnick wrote in the *Journal of the American Medical Association* in 1997:

Social science has also begun to suggest that religion, a subject that social scientists are notoriously reluctant to touch, has a significant effect, independent of economic status, in keeping children out of trouble. Evidence has begun to accumulate that in the inner city, church-going males are less likely to commit crimes than are others of the same economic status. There is evidence, suggestive though not yet conclusive, that religious programs in prison reduce criminal recidivism for prison inmates more than what one would find among similar inmates in the same prison. We do not know whether fostering religion in a child or supporting the youth-saving work of churches will produce the same effects that we now observe in the simple connection between religiosity and decency. But religiosity and decency are correlated; in time, we may learn that the former causes the latter.

Joseph Califano was Secretary of Health and Human Services during Jimmy Carter's presidency. He is now chairing the CASA project. Speaking to the importance of religion in a child's life, he also, by implication, reinforces what I've already said about the relative unimportance of after-school activities.

Religion is a key factor in giving our children the moral values, skill and will to say "no" to illegal drugs, alcohol and cigarettes. . . . If parents take their children to religious services beginning at a very early age they can have a major impact on whether or not their children resist these substances. . . . Parental involvement is a critical protective factor. The more often teens eat dinner with their parents, the less likely they are to smoke, drink or use marijuana.

Every successful culture has been built upon a strong foundation of religious values, and every culture, in its decline, has abandoned religious values and replaced them with secular ones. Religious values provide guideposts for living a good and righteous life, not to mention the strength to "just say no" to a myriad of temptations, including the temptation to resolve conflict by resorting to violence.

12

Be a Family,
a Real Family

Therefore shall a man leave his father
and his mother, and shall cleave unto his wife;
and they shall be one flesh.

—Genesis 2:24 AV

I ASKED A recent audience, some 450 strong, "I can virtually guarantee that, by making one simple decision, you can reduce parenting stress by more than half, create a more relaxed, harmonious family environment, and provide your children with more carefree childhoods. Raise your hand if that sounds good to you."

It looked to me as if everyone raised a hand.

"Okay, here's the deal," I continued. "Tell each of your children he or she can participate in only one after-school activity or program, including a church youth group, at a time. If you have more than one child, tell them their combined activities cannot take up more than two weekday afternoons and Saturday morning, nor can any activity or program interfere with dinner, which will be at home nearly every evening, with everyone present. Furthermore, tell them there'll be no activities or programs during the summer months. The summer is for the family. Do I have any takers?"

No one raised a hand. There was total silence. Four hundred and fifty pairs of eyes just stared at me, as if I'd proposed they join me in committing mass suicide. Come to think of it, to the contemporary American parent the idea of taking one's children out of all after-school activities *is* probably akin to committing parental suicide.

I've yet to find a good counter argument to my proposal. One answer I hear is that children enjoy these activities, and how can a parent tell a child he can't do something that's fun? Well, you just say, "You can't do everything you want to do." It's really that simple. Aren't the needs of the family unit more important than what children want or like? When your children are no longer children, no one is going to make sure they get to do whatever they like. And the family would benefit greatly from parents who are relaxed instead of in almost constant "hurry-up-we-gotta-go" mode.

Let's face it, children do not *need* these activities and programs. They are add-ons to an already good life. In 99 percent of cases, the activities a child is enrolled in today are going to be irrelevant to anything he or she is doing at age thirty. Furthermore, if they are not enrolled in these activities, they will probably be doing the same thing at age thirty, and just as successfully. I once said as much to a small group, and an audience member rejoined, "But what if Tiger Woods's parents hadn't started him in golf so early?"

I answered, "Then Tiger might have grown up to become a virologist, and maybe he would have discovered a cure for AIDS."

Let's face it. Tiger Woods is not making a great and wonderful contribution to mankind. It's a sad comment on our collectively misplaced values that the average American regards athletes like Tiger—a nice fellow, presumably—as heroes.

Someone might well ask, "But what if my son has a lot of innate talent for music, and I never let him develop that talent?"

Remember, I didn't say take your kids out of *all* after-school programs; rather, let each of them choose one. If your son has a lot of musical talent, and he values music as much as you value his talent, he'll choose some musical program as his one activity. And if he doesn't choose what you'd choose for him, he will take his talents (there's no such thing as having simply *one* talent, you know) and use them in some other area. And by the time he's forty years old, there's little doubt he'll be as successful in whatever path he's chosen as he would have been if he had walked the path you, with your good intentions, chose for him.

Here's another guarantee: The more relaxed the family unit, the fewer discipline problems you'll have to deal with. Furthermore, the less stress you're under, the more relaxed will be your approach to discipline. So by taking your children out of after-school activities, you'll have better behaved children. With more discretionary time, they'll be better able to focus on homework and need less "help" (aka enabling) from you. They'll even have time for chores. Oh, happy day! Children who are actually earning their keep and acquiring a solid service ethic at the same time!

Here's yet another guarantee: Less focus on children, combined with a generally more relaxed family atmosphere and definitely more relaxed parents, translates to a stronger marriage. No reasonable person would argue that being relaxed lends itself to better communication and intimacy. And please understand that there is nothing so important to the health of a family as the health of the marriage. Before you single parents out there have a conniption fit, be assured I'm not saying that single-parent families can't be healthy. I'm simply asserting an undeniable truth: If you're married with children, the health of your family depends fundamentally on the health of your marriage.

So, how about it? What a wonderful world it would be if the typical American family's number-one after-school pastime was "Let's just relax and enjoy our happy home."

"So, John," someone recently asked, "I can't help but wonder whether or not your children, when they were kids, participated in anything except family activities."

As a matter of fact, family *was* their number-one after-school activity. Eric, now thirty-one, played peewee football until the coach decided to make him starting quarterback. He promptly asked us if he could quit, explaining, "Everyone's out to get the quarterback, and I'm scared I'll get hurt." We let him quit, but he had to tell the coach himself. He then played soccer for half a season and again asked us if he could quit. He was having no fun, he said, because the coach took winning too seriously. So did the other kids' parents, he added. We agreed with his analysis, so he quit, again telling the coach himself. That is the total history of Eric and after-school activities, except for the fact that, as a teenager, he joined and participated in a Christian youth group.

Amy, now twenty-seven, wanted piano lessons. We bought her a piano with the understanding that, because of the investment required, she had to take piano lessons as long as she lived in our home. But, we added, she didn't have to practice unless she wanted to. Practice was between her and her teacher. Amy took her last piano lesson her last semester in high school. She also landed roles in a handful of community theater productions during her pre- and early teen years. She also participated in the Christian youth group.

Willie and I have witnessed what happens to families when children's after-school activities dominate a family's discretionary time. The parents never seem to have time for themselves or their marriages; they frequently complain of exhaustion and stress (as if the exhaustion and stress were not the result of choices they had made); and everyone in the family always seems to be in a constant state of hurry.

Our children, we decided, were going to look back on a family life that had been relaxed and relatively carefree. We were going to put family first, second, and third. As a consequence, we were marriage-centered, not child-centered. Eric and Amy did chores (*most* of the housework, in fact, from ages nine and six until they left for college), did their own homework, and developed hobbies with which to occupy their spare time. We didn't watch much television. In fact, for much of their childhoods, we didn't *have* a television. The things we did together were active things, things that make for good childhood memories.

Eric is now married with two children. He flies jets for a major corporation. He spends his time off with his family. He and Nancy and the boys live two doors down from us in Gastonia, North Carolina. There's nothing more important to Eric than his marriage and the family he and Nancy are creating. Willie and I couldn't be more proud of his values. He quit peewee football and he quit soccer, but Eric is anything but a quitter, as shown by the fact that he paid for most of his flight training himself and was flying jets at age twenty-four—one of the youngest (if not *the* youngest) non-military-trained jet pilots in the 1990s.

Amy is a homemaker and a new mother. She does some part-time work for me out of her home, but although she's well educated, intelligent, and has very marketable skills, she'd rather be at home building a family than doing anything else. Willie and I couldn't be more proud of her.

The ultimate joy of parenthood is watching a child grow into an adult with good, solid, traditional values—a good citizen, in other words. As Grandma said, "Good citizenship begins at home." Not the soccer field, mind you. At home.

13

Be a Dad,
a Real Dad

*And, ye fathers, provoke not your children
to wrath, but bring them up in the nurture
and admonition of the Lord.*

—Ephesians 6:4 AV

THERE ARE predictable differences in the ways mothers and fathers relate to and interact with their children. These differences have to do with biology, psychology, cultural expectations, and practical considerations. For example, in every culture mothers have usually occupied the role of primary caretaker during infancy and early childhood. This arrangement has been dictated by necessity as well as by the fact that females are generally more nurturing than males.

During the first two years of a child's life, the father functions as a "parenting aide," serving as the mother's assistant. He assists in her nearly full-time child-care ministry and relieves her when she needs a break. Despite the increased attention given to "fathering" in the last decade, the exceptions to this rule are still few and far between and, I suspect, always will be.

Of necessity, as we have seen, the typical mother is enmeshed with her child during infancy and early toddlerhood. Between her child's second and third birthdays, however, she begins to step back and away, expecting her child to act more independently. In the process, the mother slowly but surely transforms herself from a caretaker into an authority figure, from a servant to a teacher of social values. As the mother's ministry of constant service draws to a close, the marriage is restored (or should be) to center stage in the family. At this point, the father's role becomes increasingly crucial to his child's success in a number of areas. Studies have shown that preschoolers, both male and female, whose fathers are actively involved in their upbringing tend to be more outgoing, adaptable, and accepting of challenge.

It is interesting to note that the increasing importance of the father's role is not limited to humans. In *Never Cry Wolf,* naturalist and author Farley Mowat gives the reader an insightful look at the wolf family, one of the few monogamous family units in the animal kingdom. When wolf cubs are young, they are never far from their mother. She protects and nurtures them until they are able to begin fending for themselves, at which point the wolf father takes over as primary parent, teaching his offspring to hunt and kill and survive in an often-hostile environment.

Several years ago, in response to a newspaper column I had written on the importance of fathers, a feminist, herself a single mom, admonished me for suggesting that single moms can't do as good a job as two married parents. She wrote, "In reality, you don't need a father at home to have appropriate male role models."

That's true, as far as it goes, but it doesn't go far enough. It has become politically incorrect to say so, but all child-rearing situations are *not* equal. As David Blankenhorn, president of the Institute for American Values and author of *Fatherless America* has meticulously documented, children reared by single moms simply do not do as well on any measure as children raised in intact family units. There are individual exceptions to this finding, of course, but the general rule is well established. In other words, while it is true that males other than fathers can be appropriate male role models, it is wrong to think the role of fathers is not unique.

But a father's mere *presence* in his children's lives is not enough. The operative term is *actively involved*. I'm speaking of a dad who is a vigorously interested participant in the child-rearing process, not a perpetual parenting aide or a guy who sits in front of the television, demanding that everyone be quiet. Children privileged with involved fathers tend to be more self-confident, outgoing, and independent. In addition, they possess generally better social skills, exhibit fewer behavior problems, and do better in school than children whose fathers are either absent or on the sidelines.

Unfortunately, close to half of the children born in the 1990s will spend a significant part of their growing years in a home without a father. Adding to this growing crisis are those divorced fathers who rarely or never see their children. As famed child psychiatrist Urie Bronfenbrenner pointed out in a 1989 UNESCO address, such children are at significantly higher risk for all manner of behavioral and educational problems, problems that often interfere with their success as adults.

There has recently been a tendency to demonize the traditional father, characterizing him as a remote, forbidding authoritarian who controlled his children through fear. This certainly doesn't help efforts to give fathers the credit they are due and restore dignity to fatherhood, nor is it generally true. Alexis de Tocqueville, author of *Democracy in America,* described the nineteenth-century American father as stern but forgiving, strong but flexible. He listened to his children and humored them, educated them as well as demanded their obedience. As Blankenhorn points out, the typical American dad has always been a hard-working paragon of traditional masculine virtues: in short, a good role model for his children, especially his sons.

As the teen years approach, the role of fathers seems to become even more crucial to good adjustment. Researchers consistently find that teenage boys with active fathers are less prone to problems with sex, drugs, or alcohol and, even when socioeconomic factors are controlled, more likely to go to college, enter successful marriages, and eventually become good dads themselves.

These days, it's impossible to have a discussion about teens without the subject of sex coming up. Indeed, the early teen years are defined by insecurities concerning identity and sexuality. Fathers can contribute much toward helping their children successfully resolve these issues. The young teenage girl is beginning to look toward males for attention and verification of her femininity. A father's caring attention and affection will go a long way toward satisfying a daughter's need for male approval, thus reducing the likelihood that she will act out her insecurities through sexual experimentation.

Similarly, a young male who enters his adolescent years without a father will often fill the vacuum by creating and then acting out a fantasy of what being a man is all about. All too often, this fantasy includes the idea that "manliness" is a matter of sexual conquest and/or aggressiveness. Again, an actively involved dad can help his son develop a more balanced view of manhood, thus mitigating the notion that sex and physical dominance are crucial to self-worth.

If you're a father, here are some ways you can have a more powerful influence on your child's life.

1. Find at least one activity you and your child can enjoy doing together: hiking, biking, tennis, coin collecting, or just walking. Then make the time to do it on a regular basis.

2. Help (but don't force!) your child to develop hobbies and get involved in a few extracurricular activities. Show interest by attending performances and sports events. If you can find the time, become a sponsor or volunteer.

3. As your child grows, work to become less the disciplinarian and more the mentor. During the teen years, remember how important it is that the two of you make the transition from parent and child to adult and adult. Take it from a dad whose children are both adults with children of their own, the teen years set long-standing precedents in the father-child relationship. Make sure they're positive ones.

4. Communicate! Always encourage your child to use you as a sounding board to talk about any personal or social issue. Make the time to talk with your teenager about the future. In all these ways, you can help your son or daughter clarify and develop a permanent set of sound, positive values.

5. Love your child's mother with all your heart. Show your child not only what being a good dad is all about but, as well, what being a good husband is all about.

Last, but by no means least, remember that a child is never too old to be told "I love you."

14

Practice Powerful Parenting

*For the commandment is a lamp and the
teaching a light, and the reproofs of
discipline are the way to life.*

—Proverbs 6:23 NJB

OVER THE LAST thirty years or so, mental-health professionals have given American parents the impression that time out (a few minutes in a chair following a misbehavior), properly used, will put an end to any discipline problem. At one time I was a true believer in time-outs. I used them with my two children, Eric and Amy, and recommended them often to parents with whom I counseled as a family psychologist. I have since come to the conclusion that *time out works with children who are already well behaved.* It does not work—not for long, anyway—with children who have developed behavior problems that are outrageous either in kind or frequency.

Big Consequences

A child who usually walks the proverbial straight and narrow but occasionally falls off the proper path needs only a nudge to get back on track, and a few minutes in a chair will be nudge enough. But a thousand nudges will not suffice to move an out-of-control child onto a path he or she has never walked. To mix my meta-phors, using time-outs to deal with outrageous misbehavior is like trying to stop a charging elephant with a flyswatter. The fact is, the outrageous requires the equally outrageous. The problem today is that parents are reluctant to employ big consequences—and I do *not* mean hurtful, cruel, or mean ones—because professional psychobabblers have intimidated them into believing that "big" discipline is psychologically harmful. Indeed, big consequences cause children great discomfort and inconvenience, which is pre-cisely the idea. But are they psychologically harmful? Not unless you think that improved behavior is bad.

A big consequence is any consequence that serves to prove, once and for all, that parents mean business—permanently. Conse-quences of this sort serve to stop a certain misbehavior from gain-ing a foothold in a family—what Grandma meant by "nipping it in the bud." A big consequence can also be used to stop a full-blown behavior problem, one that's already beyond bud stage, in its tracks. Grandma referred to this as "lowering the boom."

Eric's Big Consequence: Two weeks into the fifth-grade school year, one of Eric's teachers called to tell us he wasn't doing his work in any of his classes. He wasn't disruptive, but he was socializing instead of working. Willie and I sat down with him and told him in no uncertain terms, "Solve this problem." In fact, we said, we trusted so much in his ability to do so that we weren't going to monitor his homework, call his teachers on a regular basis, or in any other way respond to this red flag.

"However, Mr. Eric," I added, "if your report card, which comes out in six weeks, says you haven't solved this problem, *we're* gonna solve it. Got that?"

He said he understood, but then that's what children always say when their backs are against the wall.

Six weeks later, his report card came out. It was awful. Once again, Willie and I sat down with him and said, "You didn't solve the problem; therefore, we must. For the next four weeks, if you're not in school or in church, you'll be in your room. You can come out to use the bathroom, do chores, eat with us, and go places with us as a family. During that time, your bedtime, even if there's no school the next day, will be seven o'clock. Lights out! In four weeks, we will request a progress report from your teachers. If even one of them indicates that you have not completely solved the problem, and we mean *completely*, we'll do this another four weeks. And Eric, let us remind you, you have nearly eight years left to live with us. We don't care if you spend those eight years in your room. Do you?"

Needless to say, he was thunderstruck. Never in his wildest fantasies did he think we'd do something so—well, outrageous. Four weeks later, when we requested the progress report, the teachers wrote: "Eric has been a completely different child, one of the best students we've ever had!"

From that day forth, any time there was the slightest inkling of a problem brewing in school all we had to say to Eric was, "Do you remember what happened in fifth grade?" and his problem would be not-so-miraculously solved.

Benson's Big Consequence: Benson was a major behavior problem both in school and at home. He was disruptive, disrespectful, and disobedient. At conferences with his fifth-grade teacher, principal, and counselor, it was repeatedly suggested that Benson had attention deficit disorder (ADD). The parents were reassured that

ADD is caused by bad genes; therefore, his behavior wasn't their fault. Benson, they were told, needed medication to help him control his impulses. His parents resisted this well-intentioned scribble for months. (Note: Contrary to what many parents of ADD children have been told, there is no scientific proof that ADD is inherited.)

"Finally," the mother told me, "we reached the limit of our tolerance for his shenanigans. Benson came home from school one day to discover a padlock on the door to his bedroom, which houses his television, computer, video-game unit, sports equipment, models, and so on. We told him he'd be allowed in his room for fifteen minutes in the morning to dress for school and for fifteen minutes in the evening to get ready for bed, which was going to be at seven-thirty every night, seven nights a week. His bed would be the sofa in the living room—most comfortable, if you ask me."

Benson was stunned, to say the least. When he threatened to report his parents for child abuse, they reminded him that he would be properly fed, properly protected from the elements, and sleeping in a bed that was much safer than his own. After all, he could only roll out of one side of it!

"But please!" Benson's parents said. "Tell whomever you like how abused you are."

This austere state of affairs would last a minimum of six weeks, they told him. During this time, he would not be allowed to participate in any after-school activity, have friends over, use the phone, watch television, or go anywhere except to accompany his parents. Furthermore, every single incident of misbehavior at school or home would add a week to his exile, and no amount of good behavior would shorten it.

"It was amazing," his mother continued. "His teacher called us several days later to tell us he'd become a completely different child. She'd never seen so much improvement so quickly. He became a model child at home as well—polite, cooperative, talkative, a general pleasure to be around."

Six weeks later, the padlock was removed from Benson's door with assurances that it would be reattached at the first hint of relapse. It's been almost a year and he has yet to fall off the wagon, which should surprise no one.

Stompanella's Big Consequence: Stompanella was five years old when her parents decided they'd had enough of her tantrums. These outbursts of outrage occurred whenever they refused her anything or insisted that she perform even the easiest tasks, like picking up her playthings. Stompanella's tantrums—screaming at the top of her lungs, falling on the floor, throwing things—had started during the "terrible twos," which had indeed been terrible. Since then, they'd gotten progressively worse. At first, she'd confined her fits to home, but as time went on she became less and less discerning as regarded her audience. When her kindergarten teacher called to express concern, Stompanella's parents acted— belatedly, but not too late.

The plan was simple. The first time Stompanella threw a fit on any given day, she'd be sent to the downstairs bathroom—safe, yet distinctly boring—and the door would be closed. When she was back in control of herself, she could emerge. The second time in twenty-four hours, she'd be sent to the bathroom and stripped of all privileges for the remainder of the day. This meant she could not watch television, go outside, or have a friend over. The third tantrum of the day would result in her spending the rest of the day in her room and going to bed immediately after supper. (This technique, which I call "Three Strikes and You're Out," works well with lots of behavior problems.) Her parents also informed her that until she was tantrum-free for a month, there would be no new toys, no new clothes (unless they were absolutely necessary), no treats, and no movies or other special events.

Consistent with the adage, things got worse before they got better, but Stompanella's parents stayed the course. Stompanella spent most of the first two weeks of the plan in her room. Finally, she got the message, and just like that her tantrums ceased. That's right, they just stopped. Oh, every once in a while, her parents would see one begin to boil up inside her, but before the first scream emerged, Stompanella would cut it off. She'd turn and stomp off to her room, her mouth sealed shut, to pout. As far as her parents were concerned, pouting represented light-years of improvement, so they wisely decided not to fight that battle.

In Eric's case, Willie and I nipped a problem in the bud by using a big consequence. In both Benson's and Stompanella's cases, their parents lowered the boom, thus putting relatively long-standing problems to rest. In all three cases, Grandma's old-fashioned discipline won over modern psychobabble, proving once again that there's nothing new under the sun.

I sometimes refer to big consequences as "memorable consequences," meaning that they take up permanent residence in a child's memory bank. When children become adults, they laugh about such things. Today, when the subject of Eric's fifth-grade problem comes up, he never fails to guffaw at the memory of the month he spent in his room.

Parents, give your children things to laugh about when they grow up!

Being Strict

I receive a fair number of letters and e-mails from people who are writing to affirm my belief that discipline is best when discipline is strict. Sometimes, someone will approach me at a speaking engagement to announce his or her membership in the Society for Disciplinary Strictness.

"I'm very strict," this person will say, with obvious pride, telling me about the many positive comments she receives from other often amazed people concerning her children's good behavior.

Unfortunately, I've recently discovered that what some people think is strict isn't strict at all. It's exhausting, obsessive, and silly, but it isn't strict.

I've had occasion to watch some of these pretenders be "strict" with their children. Here's a composite example of how they corrupt the term.

"Rambo! Give me that!"

Rambo, age seven, acts oblivious.

"Rambo! *Did you hear me?*"

"Yes."

"Well?"

"I'm just playing with it."

"I don't care. Give it to me. It's not a toy."

"But, Mom!"

"No! Give it to me."

"Just let me play with it for a while. Please."

"No! Now!" Mom holds her hand out expectantly.

Rambo jerks the "toy" back, away from Mom's hand.

"Rambo! Give me that! Now!"

I think you get the picture. This game may go on for two or three minutes before Mom wins, Rambo succeeds in persuading her to let him play with "it" for a while longer, or Dad intervenes and Rambo immediately hands it over. I don't mean to imply that the so-called "strict" parent is always Mom. It might be Dad. It might be both Mom and Dad.

Not so long ago, parents of the above sort were known as nags. Other parents—truly strict ones—rolled their eyes at them. In those days, however, most parents *were* strict. Today, most parents are anything but strict. In addition to nags, today's parents are wimps, bullies, soulmates, playmates, bedmates, servants, absents, and codependents. There are very few true stricts.

To illustrate truly strict, I'll return to my example, giving it a new outcome.

"Rambo, please hand that over to me. It isn't a toy."

Rambo acts oblivious.

Mom, without any show or feeling of anger, takes Rambo by the hand, leads him to his bedroom, and says, "You're going to be in here for one hour, young man. Furthermore, I'm calling off your spend-the-night with Billy. You can spend the night at his house some other time."

"Mom! Okay! I'm sorry!"

"That's fine, but your apology doesn't change the fact that you didn't do what I told you to do."

"Mom! It's not fair!"

"Rambo, you're a very smart boy, smart enough to figure out that when I talk to you I mean business. I'm certainly not going to insult your intelligence by repeating myself. Now, I'll let you know when your hour is up." Mom walks away.

And that's that. I think you get the picture, but just in case: Strict is letting a child know that words are not simply exhalations of hot air. They mean something. Strict isn't mean (although children sometimes *think* it is), loud, threatening, or even punitive. My consistent personal and professional experience is that strict parents, because they convince their children that words mean something, punish less and enjoy their children more.

A parent once told me she felt I placed too much emphasis on the need to be strict and not enough on the need to be relaxed and affectionate with children. She said it was her experience that a relaxed parent disciplines more effectively.

I agree, but I would turn that around: *Parents who discipline their children effectively are the most relaxed parents.*

The most essential element of successful discipline is good communication, not correct selection of consequences for misbehavior. As any public speaker will attest, the more relaxed someone is, the better communicator he or she will be. Good disciplinary communication saves words. It's straightforward, to the point, and commanding (as opposed to demanding). I call it Alpha-speech, meaning that it is communication befitting a confident leader, in this case a leader of children.

For example, if a mother wants her son to pick up his toys, she should simply say, "It's time for you to pick up these toys." Then, in keeping with Grandma's wise observation that "a watched pot never boils," the mother should walk away.

Alpha-speech prevents discipline problems—not completely, but significantly. As dog trainers will confirm, the discipline of a dog is primarily a matter of how the dog's master gives commands.

Again, the key is not punishment but communication. Good communication will prevent up to 90 percent of behavior problems. The remaining 10 percent require that the child experience consequences. That's where the need to be strict comes in.

Strict discipline is powerful but not harsh. It is consistent but not necessarily predictable or repetitious. For these reasons, strict discipline puts a quick end to problems. Thus, it is in the best interests of both parent and child.

Continuing with my example, let's say the boy ignores his mother's command to pick up his toys. I'd advise her to pick up the toys calmly herself and then tell her son that, because of his obstinance, he will go to bed immediately after the evening meal. He protests, cries, pleads. The mother holds fast. Two weeks later, the child ignores another command and is informed that he will not be allowed to play in that day's soccer game. He protests, cries, pleads. The mother holds fast. It's another three months before this child ignores a parental instruction. By being strict, the parent has made a disciplinary molehill out of a potential disciplinary mountain. The child is more well behaved, and the parent is under less stress; therefore, she is more relaxed and able to be more spontaneously, genuinely affectionate.

In other words, relaxation is the payoff for being an effective disciplinarian.

Strong Love

Parents who read parenting books are concerned, conscientious, caring, and committed. They are certainly well intentioned, but that doesn't mean they are doing the right things. They undoubtedly love their children, but not all love is equal. Just as it is possible to discipline wrongly, it is possible to love wrongly. Many well-intentioned parents, unfortunately, love their children deeply and wrongly at the same time. Like their discipline, their love is weak rather than strong.

Weak love is indulgent, permissive, appeasing. Parents who love weakly generally expect a lot of themselves and relatively little of their children. They want their children to make good grades in school, but they ensure the good grades by sitting with each child as he or she does his homework, guiding every move. In so doing, they harm their children more than help them, out of misplaced love. Weak love is also afraid of making a child upset, afraid of hearing the child yell either "You don't love me!" or "I hate you!"

By contrast, strong love is empowering, *but a child may not always like it.* The parent whose love is strong understands that children must learn certain things the hard way, through relatively lonely encounters with adversity, by making mistakes and learning from them. Strong love is there to protect but realizes that adversity per se is not reason enough for protection.

Strong love helps a child stand on his own two feet, requires that a child lie in the beds he makes, lets a child stew in his own juices, and is supportive but requires that a child fight his own battles. Weak love, on the other hand, props a child up, lies in the child's beds, stews in the child's juice, and fights the child's battles.

Here's a story about strong love: My mother possesses a PhD in plant morphology, an esoteric life science. She is brilliant, and her brilliance extends to matters of math. One day when I was in the fifth grade or thereabouts, I came to her complaining about a math problem that was giving me trouble. She looked at my math book, noted that the concept was still being taught the way she learned it, and handed the book back to me.

"I figured this out when I was your age," she said. "You can too."

"Mom!" I protested. "I've been working on it for almost thirty minutes!"

"Oh," she replied, "you're telling that to the wrong person. I've been working on some problems for five *years* now and still haven't solved them."

And with that, Mom dismissed me with an imperious gesture remindful of the Queen of England. My foolish eleven-year-old heart hated my mother for that. I remember storming away, saying something along the lines of "You don't even care!" In fact, Mom cared enough to not always make everything better. She forced me to learn that I was capable of solving my own problems. She already knew that, but I needed to find out for myself.

You can't bring out the best in your children by just telling them that they're capable. You have to make them discover their capabilities, and doing that requires that they struggle, courtesy of parents who support them but do not struggle *for* them. Strong love, tough love—you can call it what you will. It's *real* love.

15

Don't Allow These
Fifteen Behaviors, Period!

For whom the Lord loves he reproves;
even as a father corrects the
son in whom he delights.

—Proverbs: 3:12 NJB

EVEN THE MOST well-behaved child is capable of outrageous misbehavior. To say this another way, any child is capable of doing something disgraceful like lying, stealing, becoming physical with a younger child, or throwing a public temper tantrum. In the face of any one of these high-stakes misbehaviors, parents should certainly take immediate and firm disciplinary action. But the fact that an otherwise fairly well-behaved child does something outrageous simply means he or she is human. Rather than any one misbehavior, it's a persistent *pattern* of misbehavior that signals trouble.

The age of the child is another consideration. Behavior that's typical of toddlers—tantrums, refusing to share, hitting or biting when mad—is a different matter entirely when the child in question is three or older. A two-year-old who bites another child in the course of struggling over a toy needs to be punished, but it cannot be said that this child has a problem. Biting is inappropriate at any age, but it does not warrant strong concern until age three.

Three years old is the age of intent. It can reasonably be said that toddlers do not truly *intend* to do some of the inappropriate things they do. Take a piece of candy away from a toddler and he may fall on the floor and scream at the top of his lungs. He doesn't *intend* to fall on the floor. At this age, a tantrum under those circumstances is reflexive. A three-year-old who throws a tantrum when he doesn't get his way knows what he's doing. His tantrum may look no different from the toddler's, but it is. Tantrums at age three are not reflexive, they are *intentionally manipulative.* The child knows that adults are likely to give in if he pitches a fit, so he pitches a fit.

Fifteen Misbehaviors

Tantrums are just one of fifteen flagrant misbehaviors which, if exhibited with a fair amount of frequency by a child three or older, signal a serious problem that should be curbed as quickly as possible. I've organized them into four categories, which, taken together, make up the criminal (psychopathological) personality: *manipulative, rebellious, aggressive,* and *deceitful.* Please don't misunderstand me. If your child is four years old and still throwing tantrums, I'm not saying he or she is a criminal in the making. I'm saying you have a serious problem on your hands and you need to stop the tantrums as fast as you can. A four-year-old who throws tantrums is very likely to be a six year-old who is belligerently defiant. A defiant six-year-old is likely to be a bully at age ten. And a ten-year-old bully is very likely to be a habitual liar by thirteen. So what begins as tantrums may end up as a serious, even life-threatening problem that becomes increasingly difficult to turn around as it gains in strength. By the teen years it may be out of control.

The more of the following behaviors a child exhibits, the more serious the problem is.

Manipulative, self-centered behavior

1. Refuses to share and becomes upset and oppositional if instructed to share by an adult.
2. Pitches fits if not "first" or given the best or is beaten in a game.
3. Reacts to another child's (including a sibling's) accomplishments with disdain, as in, "So? I can do it better."
4. Throws temper tantrums in reaction to an instruction or the word *no*.

Rebellious behavior

5. Consistently ignores or defies specific adult instructions.
6. Deliberately and consistently breaks rules (e.g., continues to ride a bike in the street after being told repeatedly not to do so).
7. Is verbally or physically disrespectful toward adults (calls names, talks back, acts mockingly, sticks out tongue).
8. Is demanding when making requests of adults.

Aggressive behavior

9. Hits, kicks, or bites other children when upset.
10. Hits or threatens to hit adults when upset.
11. Is cruel to animals.

12. Bullies other children (uses physical advantage to intimidate and overpower others, threatens other children with harm if they don't cooperate).

Destructive, deceitful behavior

13. Steals from parents, siblings, playmates, other people's houses, or stores.
14. Vandalizes or deliberately destroys other people's property, including other children's toys and possessions.
15. Lies consistently to avoid responsibility for misbehavior, even when evidence of his or her culpability is obvious.

The obvious question is: *How should parents deal with each of these behaviors in a child three or older?* Note that in each of the following case examples, punishment is accompanied by an explanation of the why and wherefore of the appropriate behavior. The fact is that when it comes to any of these misbehaviors, punishment alone works no better than explanation alone. *What works is punishment accompanied by explanation.* Generally, the explanation should *follow* the punishment for the simple reason that a child is oftentimes too upset at the moment a punishment is delivered to listen to the explanation. Reasons should be given after the child has calmed down, not in the heat of the moment. In some cases, after giving an appropriate explanation on several separate occasions, future explanations are unnecessary. Whether or not the child has heard enough explanations is a judgment call.

1. Refuses to share: Take the toy away until the child shows a readiness to play more cooperatively. If he becomes upset when the toy is taken, isolate him in a suitable time-out place until self-control is restored. When the child has calmed down, explain that sharing is the same as helping, and that both are what friends do. If we want to make friends, we share and we help one another.

2. Pitches fits when he's not first or loses a game: Isolate the child in the bedroom or away from the play group until he's calmed down and will sit and listen. Explain that it's okay to want to be first and to want to win, but it's very bad manners to get upset if you're not first or if you lose. Say that as long as he gets upset at not being first, you will not allow him to be first, ever, and you will remove him from the group at the first sign of a blowup. Furthermore, you will remove him if you see that he is winning! You will not let him win at anything until he has learned to lose without losing control. Where losing is concerned, explain that the correct thing to do when someone else wins a game is to offer congratulations. Given the immature behavior often exhibited by today's professional athletes, a child who becomes upset at losing should not be allowed to watch professional sports on television—not just hockey and wrestling, but *any* professional sport.

3. Reacts to another child's accomplishments with disdain: Insist that your child apologize to the other child. If he refuses, make him sit alone in some boring place like the dining room until he says he's willing to apologize, and sincerely so. If the apology doesn't sound sincere, refuse to accept it and send him back to the boring place until he's ready to give it another try. Point out how bad he would feel if another child said what he just said. So just as he likes praise from others, so should he praise, or at least congratulate, other children's acomplishments.

4. Throws temper tantrums: A relatively mild tantrum (crying) can be dealt with by simply assigning the child to a suitably boring area until control is regained. If the tantrum is destructive (throwing things, attempting to hit), the area in which the child is confined must be one that does not provide any opportunity to destroy anything or where the only things he can destroy belong to him (e.g., in his room). In the latter instance, when the tantrum is over, the child is not allowed out until everything is back in order. If something has been broken that belongs to someone else, even a parent or sibling, the child must apologize *and* make restitution by either giving away a possession or doing something out of the ordinary for the person whose possession was destroyed. Go back over the situation that brought on the tantrum and talk about how the child could have handled it differently.

5. Consistently ignores or defies adult instructions: This should never, ever, be tolerated! In the case of a three-year-old, every *single* occurrence should result in a time-out period of at least fifteen minutes. (Time out generally works with three-year-olds.) Time out should take place in a relatively isolated area, such as a thoroughly childproofed bathroom, a vestibule, or a staircase, and a timer should be used to signal when the child is released. The child should not receive or be able to obtain attention from others during this time. If the occurrence takes place outside the home, time out should be administered on the spot if a suitable place is available or can be quickly improvised. Otherwise, time out can wait until the child is home. In the case of a child who is older than three, time out should be used for the first two occurrences of any given day. On the third occurrence, send the child to his or her room for the remainder of the day, cancel all remaining activities, and put the child to bed at least one hour early, if not immediately after dinner. It goes without saying that the child's room should be comfortable but not a self-contained "entertainment complex" with a television, computer, video games, or stereo. Explain to the child that everyone—you included—has to obey rules. When people don't obey rules, they are punished. Give examples: such as when someone incurs a speeding ticket or is fired from a job. Tell the child that one of the rules of the family is that children must do what parents tell them to do, every single time they are told. If they disobey, they must be punished.

6. Deliberately breaks rules: Handle as in number 5.

7. Is verbally or physically disrespectful toward adults: This would include name-calling (e.g., "You're stupid!"), making obscene gestures, or saying outrageous things like "I'm going to kill you!" (I do not include "I hate you!" in this category. In my estimation, this is not actually disrespectful, in that it refers to the child's feelings in the heat of the moment rather than being directly insulting of the adult in question. However, a child should not be allowed to yell "I hate you!" in a public area or when there are guests present.) For a three-year-old, a time-out is appropriate. When the time is up, the child must apologize in order to obtain release or continue to sit until he or she is ready to apologize. For a child four and older, the third such occurrence on any given day should result in being confined to his or her room for the remainder of the day, awaiting an early bedtime. The child can only come out to use the bathroom, eat meals with the family, do regularly assigned chores, and go places with the family. Simply explain that names, obscenities, and gestures are hurtful of other people's feelings and cannot be allowed, much less simply ignored. Parents who feel comfortable doing so should also point out that the Ten Commandments require children to be respectful of their parents. In the case of the older child who is being confined, early bedtime can be suspended if the child is willing to apologize to the offended party. It is also appropriate to "parole" an older child from room confinement if he produces a suitable written apology.

8. Is demanding toward adults: Handle as in number 5. Explain to the child that it is rude to demand things of people.

9. Hits, kicks, or bites other children when upset: Parents *must* adopt a no-tolerance policy toward these forms of aggression and toward misbehaviors 10 through 15. A child under three should be confined to his or her room for one hour, and all of that day's remaining privileges and activities should be canceled. For a child three or older the first aggressive outburst on any given day should result in room confinement for the remainder of the day and an early bedtime. Needless to say, all remaining privileges and activities, including organized sports, should be canceled. If the problem occurs on a daily basis, the third time it occurs in any given week a child four or older should be confined for the remainder of the week with *all* extracurricular activities canceled—yes, even if the team will suffer. Stopping aggression toward others is infinitely more important than a soccer game.

10. Hits or threatens to hit adults: Same as number 9. I must add, however, that I have no problem with spanking a child who hits parents, siblings, or other children. The spanking should occur immediately and be followed by an appropriate period of confinement as described. There is no evidence that a spanking under such circumstances is "confusing" to a child. Nor is there evidence that spankings per se play any role in the development of violent tendencies. To use another example: Many elderly people (pre-modern parents, therefore) to whom I've spoken attest to curing their children of biting by biting them back. These "cures" were usually immediate. One bite to the biter was all it took. Recall that my grandson Patrick was "cured" of hitting with one swift swat to his buttocks. (For more on spanking, see chapter 6.)

11. Is cruel to animals: Same as in number 9. Again, I have no problem with spanking a young child for cruelty to animals. This is highly predictive of later, extremely serious antisocial behavior and must be stopped as quickly as possible.

12. Bullies other children: Same as in number 9.

13. Steals: My professional experience has convinced me that stealing is potentially addictive, and powerfully so. The child who steals and gets away with it is likely to steal again and again. Every successful theft lends that much more drive to the child's compulsion. For this reason, a child can go from being completely honest to being a thoroughly addicted thief in a matter of weeks. The child who has become a compulsive thief *must never be given the benefit of doubt where stealing is concerned.* If something is missing and parents are reasonably sure the item has not simply been misplaced, it must be assumed the child stole the item. In that event, all privileges and extracurricular activities, including participation in athletic events, should be suspended until the child returns the item and issues an apology to the victim. Explain that, in the larger world, some of the most severe criminal penalties are given to people who steal. Moreover, stealing is specifically proscribed in the Ten Commandments. "Thou shall not steal" is one of mankind's oldest and most important laws.

14. Deliberately destroys other people's property: This is really no different from stealing and should be handled similarly. In this case, the child should be confined to the home with all privileges and activities suspended until he or she apologizes and comes up with an appropriate plan for making restitution to the victim. For example, if a five-year-old destroys another child's toy, let the victim take any toy he or she chooses from the guilty child's toy collection. Explain this the same way one would explain the prohibition against stealing.

15. Lies to avoid responsibility: When it is discovered that a child has lied to avoid punishment or censure, he should experience a punishment appropriate to the original offense and an additional punishment for lying. Depending on the severity of the original offense (which determines the severity of the lie), the child can be confined for the remainder of the day or longer, and privileges and activities can be suspended for an appropriate period of time. He should also be required to come forth with a verbal or written apology. The preschool child should simply be told that lying is against the rules. A school-age child should be told that (a) mutual trust is based on telling the truth and that breaking a bond of trust is hurtful and (b) telling the truth, even when it's going to get you into trouble, is a mark of being grown up. Say that, yes, it's hard, but doing the right thing is often difficult.

16

Media Violence, Bullies, and Your Child

Rescue me, Yahweh, from evil men,
protect me from violent men,
whose heart is bent on malice.

—Psalm 140:1–2 NJB

DURING THE WRITING of this book, I happened to mention my subject matter to a Japanese friend. I told him that some people think television and video-game violence causes children to become violent. He smiled and remarked that the content of much of the television watched and the video games played by Japanese children is violent. Yet Japanese children are decidedly nonviolent, especially when compared with American children.

"Parents in America," he pointed out, "have to explain violence to children. In my country, violence is regarded as largely a fantasy thing. The violence that children see (on television and in video games) has nothing to do with reality, so there's no need to explain it to them. But here, the stuff that kids see in cartoons they also see on the six o'clock news."

Yes, he's right. Because violence is not simply a "fantasy thing" in America, and because children are going to figure this out sooner or later, American parents must stand ready to explain violence to their kids, to try and put it in proper perspective.

    1. The explanation should be appropriate to the child's age and take into account what the child *needs* to know. It is important, regardless of what one is explaining to a child, to take care not to frighten or condescend unnecessarily.

    2. Be mindful of the child's life circumstances. Obviously, a child who lives in the inner city needs more information about violence than does a child who lives in an Amish community. But again, the bottom line is answered by the question, "What does this child *need* to know?"

Unlike some of my colleagues in the mental-health professions, I do not believe that the child who asks a question always deserves an answer. Nor do I think that simply because a child has witnessed something—a violent act, for example—that some adult should necessarily explain it. Put another way, I think it is perfectly appropriate to tell children, young ones in particular, "You are not old enough to truly understand the answer to your question, so I want you to put it aside and ask me again in a few years." Children not only accept responses of that sort but are also satisfied by them. We adults tell children entirely too much these days. We give them too many explanations, and in many cases the explanations create more problems than they solve. They confuse, create undue anxiety, and often result in fears that keep children up at night.

    Regarding violence and its effect on children, the two issues that arise most often, and which I'm going to deal with in the following pages, are violence in the media and real violence by bullies.

Violence in the Media

On April 3, 2000, *Time* magazine ran a letter from a San Francisco mother of a six-year-old girl. The child had asked if a Michigan six-year-old boy who had recently shot and killed a classmate would be put in jail. The mother said she tried her best to explain why he would not be punished and ended her letter: "Although I am glad my daughter is developing a healthy respect for life, I am still grappling with the reality of having had this conversation at all."

I wondered how the child knew about this horrible event in the first place. My grandson Jack, age five at the time, did not know about it. His parents do not allow him to watch television news, which is often a parade of carnage and mayhem from around the world. Television news is skewed to the negative, and its immediacy and authenticity may well give a young child the notion that the event being portrayed happened just around the corner. Forced to choose between letting a six-year-old watch Arnold Schwarzenegger in *The Terminator* or the six o'clock news, I'd opt for the former. Mind you, I'm describing a hypothetical situation in which I *have* to choose. Actually, I wouldn't let a child younger than thirteen watch *The Terminator*. Even then, I wouldn't let a child view this movie or others like it if the child had a tendency to be fearful or obsessive or had a history of being physically aggressive toward peers or siblings.

Quite simply, the solution to violence in the media is not to let children watch television unless the programs are carefully screened beforehand. If that isn't possible and there's some question as to the content of a program, don't let the child watch it. One solution is to let children watch only programs that are guaranteed by the network to be free of violence and sex.

If your child is exposed to violent media and has questions, again, answer conservatively. If the child is old enough to be given an answer, be brief and reassuring.

Don't, for example, say to a six-year-old: "The boys who shot those people were bad boys who live in troubled families where people probably argued and fought all the time." By age six children already know some bad kids, but the ones they know are probably not bad enough to start shooting people. Also, the explanation may cause the child to become unduly frightened the next time an argument occurs in the family.

Do say, "The boys who shot those people live far away. Nothing like that is going to happen around here." Notice, the six-year-old in question is not given an explanation. He or she is simply reassured that this is nothing to worry about.

Someone might ask, "But John! How can the parents be sure something like that *isn't* going to happen in their community?"

They can't. But a six-year-old doesn't need to know that. That knowledge would serve absolutely no purpose and would simply cause the child to fret.

Needless to say, I'd be more truthful with a nine-year-old, but I'd still reassure the child that "nothing of that sort is going to happen around here." Children simply do not need to know that such things could happen in their school until they are old enough to deal with that level of truthfulness without obsessing, around twelve or thirteen. No sooner, even if the child in question is extremely intelligent. Intelligence does not make a child immune to anxiety. Overly complicated, explicit explanations can frighten even intelligent children.

So where media violence is concerned, protect your children from it as much as possible, for as long as possible. And when questions arise, answer them with utmost respect for the child's age and innocence.

Violence by Bullies

As I pointed out in the introduction, anecdotal and survey evidence strongly suggests bullying is becoming more of a problem in America's schools and neighborhoods. A survey conducted by the Parents' Resource Institute for Drug Education (PRIDE) found that one in five children in grades six through twelve report having been hit, slapped, or kicked while at school; one in four report having been fearful of aggression from another child; two in five have perpetrated or threatened aggression toward peers. Dorothy Espelage, a psychologist at the University of Illinois, says those numbers would be higher still if what she terms "relational bullying"—name-calling and teasing—were counted as well. Espelage conducted a study in which relational bullying was included and found that, in one thirty-day period, eight out of ten children had bullied a classmate.

Bullying is not just a problem for children, however. Of all parenthood's trials, perhaps the most vexing is discovering that your child has become the target of a bully. Every time an incident occurs, you feel overwhelmed by a paralyzing maelstrom of emotions, including anger (sometimes bordering on rage), despair, frustration, and guilt.

Bullies tend to select victims who aren't likely to retaliate or even defend themselves against the physical and emotional insults that are a bully's stock-in-trade. A "target child" is typically small for his or her age, quiet, sensitive, and well-liked by adults—a child who "wouldn't hurt a flea." Although not necessarily unpopular with other children, the bully's victim rarely can claim a lot of friends. Consequently, other children aren't likely to come to his or her defense.

Further complicating matters is the fact that a bully's parents often deny the problem. If confronted by other parents or teachers, they are likely to defend their child or rationalize the behavior. Because bullies are rarely held accountable and are often protected from consequences, their aggressive acts tend to become increasingly outrageous, if not dangerous, over time. (Note: I'm deliberately avoiding the male pronoun. Bullying by females is also on the rise.)

When occasional taunting turns into conscious harassment, it's time for parents to step in. But what's a parent to do? If you complain to school authorities, the school may do nothing, especially if the school in question is a public school where, as pointed out in chapters 1 and 8, teachers and administrators often will not discipline for fear of lawsuits. Furthermore, the bully may find out about the complaint and become that much more determined to hurt your child. If you complain to the bully's parents, you'll probably run into a brick wall. You can increase your protection of your child, but for how long and at what expense to your child's freedom and self-confidence? You can stay out of it, but doesn't that amount to throwing your child to the wolf?

There are several important things to keep in mind when deciding how to help your child deal with a bully.

- Any direct intervention on your part may backfire. Bullies become even more determined when adults get involved.
- Bullies can't be reasoned with. They tend to be very troubled children with poor self-concepts, poor social skills, and tu-

multuous family situations. Most of them are starved for affection and acceptance.

- Bullies *do* understand force. If all else fails, consider asking law-enforcement authorities to get involved.
- The bullying should be stopped as quickly as possible. The longer it continues the longer it will take for the victim's emotional scars to heal. Also, some target children eventually begin expressing their anger toward younger and smaller children.

Here are three examples of how parents I know have successfully handled bullying situations.

Book 'em, Danno! Ten-year-old Robbie's parents decided to handle the problem the same way they would if an adult assaulted one of them. Having suffered along with Robbie for nearly a year, during which he was the frequent target of a much bigger and very troubled classmate, they finally filed a complaint with the police. The bully was arraigned in juvenile court and released to the custody of his parents. At the same time, an attorney informed the bully's parents that if the problem continued they would be sued for damages. They bully was ultimately placed on probation, and the entire family was ordered to see a court-appointed psychologist. The bully never again even looked in Robbie's direction.

Change schools. Franklin was twelve when the harassment began. His tormentor would sit behind him on the bus and pull his hair or thump him on his head. At school, the bully intimidated Franklin into letting him copy work. Franklin began to develop stomachaches and headaches. His parents talked to the principal about the problem but were told there was little the school could do. The principal did consent to contact the bully's parents and speak with them, but like 99.9 percent of parents of bullies, they refused to admit there was a problem. The principal finally suggested that Franklin transfer to a different school in the district. Despite the inconvenience and the injustice, Franklin's parents agreed, bringing that chapter in their lives to a close.

Keep away. Derek's parents tried another approach. They coached him on how to avoid his antagonist, a boy who was two years ahead of Derek in school. Derek took a different route home from school every day, stayed close to teachers on the playground, ignored the bully's taunts, and went inside the minute the bully appeared in the neighborhood. Eventually, the boy lost interest in Derek.

The very best solution, of course is for the bully and his or her parents to begin working with a therapist. Unfortunately, this requires that the parents recognize the problem and assume their share of responsibility for it. In the final analysis, a bully's behavior reflects underlying family problems that aren't going to be resolved by either punishment or counseling alone.

17

Final Words

*The fear of the Lord is the beginning
of knowledge; but fools despise
wisdom and instruction.*

—Proverbs 1:7 AV

In CLOSING, it might be helpful to review my recommendations.

- Teach your children well, beginning with their manners. Good manners are a show of respect for others, and respect for others is the key to strength of character.
- Put family ahead of individual children. Limit extracurricular activities so your children, especially during their early and middle years, spend most of their free time with the family, doing family-oriented things. Remember what Grandma said. "Good citizenship begins at home!"
- Fathers should get involved with their children, always keeping in mind that their interest and guidance are especially significant to the social and emotional health of both sons and daughters. Every father should be a "fisher of children."
- Discipline your children powerfully. Not harshly or with anger, but with firmness and strength of purpose—the purpose being to put them on the path that leads through the narrow

gate to which Jesus referred in Matthew 7:14. Nip misbehavior in the bud. Let children learn their lessons the hard way, by discovering that for every choice there is a consequence. Hold them responsible for their behavior. Allow no excuses, no ifs, ands, or buts.

- Do not allow violent media into your home. You wouldn't let rats, roaches, or any other filthy infestation into your house, so don't allow the infestation of violence in the media. Just as you wouldn't let your children consume dirty food, don't allow them to consume filth and violence in the media.

- Love your children with as much strength of purpose as you discipline them. Let them lie in the beds they make, fight their own battles, paddle their own canoes. In these ways, you help them learn to stand on their own two feet.

It's not rocket science, folks. It's just good old common sense.

Coda

In a May 27, 1999, letter to the editor of the *Charlotte Observer*, a teacher describes asking his high school civics class what could justify going to school and killing a classmate. To his horror, the students reeled off an "enthusiastic" litany of reasons, including "someone dissing you," "a guy taking your girl," and "someone embarrassing you." The teacher, a Vietnam vet, astutely commented, "The problem we have is not with guns, it's with what has happened to kids."

It's true. And what's happened to kids is narcissism unbound, punishments undelivered, violence-obsessed media, irrational laws, love that is weak, and mental-health professionals who have become little more than professional enablers.

References and Suggested Readings

American Academy of Pediatrics. "The Short- and Long-Term Consequences of Corporal Punishment." *Pediatrics,* October 1996, 801–860.

American Psychological Association. "Family and Relationships: Children and Television Violence" (undated article downloaded from APA Web site, 1999).

Albuquerque Public Schools. "Individuals with Disabilities Education Act (IDEA) Reauthorization: Changes in Discipline." September 1999.

Baumeister, Roy F., et al. "Relation of Threatened Egotism to Violence and Aggression: The Dark Side of High Self-Esteem." *Psychological Review,* vol. 103, no. 1 (1996), 5–33.

Baumrind, Diana. "The Development of Instrumental Competence Through Socialization." *Minnesota Symposium on Child Psychology,* vol. 7, no. 35 (1993).

Blankenhorn, David. *Fatherless America.* New York: Harperperennial Library, 1996.

"Bullies Shove Their Way into the Nation's Schools." *USA Today,* September 7, 1999. Life Section, page 1.

Charen, Mona. "How We've Failed Our Children." *Conservative Chronicle,* November 11, 1999.

Czudner, Gad. *Small Criminals Among Us: How to Recognize and Change Children's Antisocial Behavior Before They Explode.* Far Hills, N.J.: New Horizon Press, 1999.

Eron, Leonard. "Relationship of TV Viewing Habits and Aggressive Behavior in Children." *Journal of Abnormal and Social Psychology*, 67, 193–196.

Gerbner, G., and N. Signorielli. "Violence Profile, 1967 Through 1988–89: Enduring Patterns." Manuscript, Annenberg School of Communications, University of Pennsylvania, 1990.

Gordon, Thomas. *Parent Effectiveness Training*. New York: Peter H. Wyden, 1970.

_____. *Teaching Children Self-Discipline at Home and at School*. New York: Times Books, 1989.

Greene, Ross. *The Explosive Child*. New York: HarperCollins, 1998.

Grossman, David, and Gloria DeGaetano. *Stop Teaching Our Kids to Kill: A Call to Action Against TV, Movie and Video Game Violence*. New York: Crown Publishers, 1999.

Healy, Jane. *Endangered Minds: Why Our Children Don't Think and What To Do About It*. New York: Simon & Schuster, 1991.

Hymowitz, Kay. *Ready or Not: Why Treating Children as Small Adults Endangers Their Future—And Ours*. Free Press, 1999.

Irwin, A. Roland, and Alan M. Gross. "Cognitive Tempo, Violent Video Games, and Aggressive Behavior in Young Boys." *Journal of Family Violence*, September 1995.

Jacobs, Joanne. "Evil, Not Rage, Drove Teen Killers." *Charlotte Observer*, November 1999 (undated download from *Charlotte Observer* Web site).

Jacobson, Simon (ed.) *Toward a Meaningful Life: the Wisdom of the Rebbe*. New York: William Morrow, 1995.

Jensen, Peter. "Television Violence Is a Cause for Concern." *Baltimore Sun*, 1999.

Kellerman, Jonathan. *Savage Spawn*. New York: Ballantine Books, 1999.

Larzelere, Robert E. "A Review of the Outcomes of Parental Use of Nonabusive or Customary Physical Punishment." *Pediatrics,* October 1996, 824–828.

Larzelere, Robert E. et al. "Nonabusive Spanking: Parental Liberty or Child Abuse?" *Children's Legal Rights Journal,* Fall 1997, 7–17.

Ledingham, Jane. "The Effect of Media Violence on Children." The National Clearinghouse on Family Violence, 1999.

Lee, Fern. "Death in the First Grade" (Letter to the Editor). *Time,* April 3, 2000, 11.

Leo, John. "Parent-free Zone." *U.S. News and World Report,* November 1, 1999.

Mowat, Farley. *Never Cry Wolf.* New York: Bantam Books, 1983.

Murray, Bridget. "Boys to Men: Emotional Miseducation." *American Psychological Association Monitor Online,* July/August 1999.

Murray, John P. "Impact of Televised Violence." Manuscript, School of Family Studies and Human Services, Kansas State University, 1999.

Newberger, Eli H. *The Men They Will Become.* Reading, Mass.: Perseus Books, 1999.

Payne, Thomas E. "Youth Violence Literature and Resource Guide." Department of Criminal Justice, The University of Mississippi—Gulf Coast, 1998.

Pollack, William. *Real Boys: Rescuing Our Sons from the Myths of Boyhood.* Owl, 1999.

Quindlen, Anna. "The C Word in the Hallways: Let's Stop Dismissing Mental Illness in Kids as a Character Flaw—Before We Have to Identify Bodies." *Newsweek,* November 29, 1999.

Samenow, Stanton. *Before It's Too Late: Why Some Kids Get Into Trouble and What Parents Can Do About It.* New York: Times Books, 1998.

Sears, William, and Martha Sears. "She is very destructive." Question answered by the Searses on parentsoup.com, downloaded on November 20, 1999.

Straus, Murray. *Beating the Devil Out of Them: Corporal Punishment in American Families.* New York: Lexington Books, 1994.

Whitehead, Barbara Dafoe, and David Popenoe. "Defining Daddy Down." *American Enterprise,* September/October 1999, 31–34.

Yeoman, Barry. "Bad Girls." *Psychology Today,* November/December 1999, 54–57, 71.

Index